**Trump was not exempt from
the jabs of tabloid television . . .**

". . . Donald, you'll remember, was having a none-too-discreet affair with a model named Marla Maples, and at a ski resort in Aspen, Ivana told the other blonde in public to keep her mitts off her husband . . .

"Through some devious means or another we obtained an exercise tape that Marla had made, which showed her jumping up and down in a clinging sweatsuit, bouncing and jiggling like mad. Every time we mentioned Trump, and we made certain to mention him a lot during that period, we showed the exercise tape . . ."

"[A] slick, entertaining memoir by a master of tabloid TV . . . a snappy account of how *A Current Affair* rose to the top."

— *Kirkus*

Current Affairs
A Life on the Edge

MAURY POVICH
WITH KEN GROSS

BERKLEY BOOKS, NEW YORK

To Connie—of course

Anyone who knows my organizational skills could testify to my lack thereof. So it is with great pleasure, indeed undying gratitude, I thank the following. To Neil Nyren, vice president, publisher, and editor in chief of Putnam's, for suggesting this book and riding herd over it. To Ken Gross, who kept me talking and writing and focused, a near-impossibility. It is he who gave the book its heart and touch. To the staff of *A Current Affair,* who made my job easy. To my assistant, Amy Sommer, who researched my memory. That took some doing. To Paul Baerwald, a thirty-year friend, for his manuscript suggestions. To my daughters, Susan and Amy, who were in my thoughts always. And to my father, who looked over everything and helped the cause by reminding me that on page 30 of the first draft I spelled my mother's name wrong. That would have been a mortal sin. Maybe she would have forgiven me. Maybe not.

Current Affairs

A
Life on the
Edge

Chapter One

I like to think of myself as a newshound from the old school. I was trained by street dogs who hung out at the cop shop and listened like night watchmen for the bulletin bells on the wire machines. Those old pros in Washington and Chicago—we'd chase fires and riots and wisps in the night. There was nothing like the chase after news.

Which is why it was hard to understand how, on the night of the biggest story of the decade, I was at the Pierre Hotel drinking cocktails in a monkey suit instead of listening for those bells. But oh, how we recovered.

It was a Thursday evening, November 9, 1989, and I was attending a black tie dinner on Manhattan's glittering Gold Coast. There was rich polished wood and thick carpets underfoot and the subdued whisper of money. Magnums of champagne and silver trays of shrimp floated through the ballroom, and I could feel the throb of the great capitalist engine as the talk of mergers and buyouts wafted like perfume through the room. It wasn't my scene, usually, but I had acquired a certain amount of celebrity as the host of *A Current Affair,* and so I had gotten invited to a few of these. They could be fun if you went to them with the right attitude.

I turned around—and there was Rupert. As he shook my hand, I could see in his eyes that he was surprised to find me there, in that place, among those people. "What are you doing here?" his eyes said. "You're supposed to be on television, not hobnobbing with the corporate commandos."

I was not easily rattled. After all, on television, my job was to interview everyone from murderers to kings. My writ ran from the gutter to the throne room. However, Rupert Murdoch, the multibillionaire Australian press baron, was my boss. And no one knew what went on behind that ambiguous expression on his face that he wore like an escape clause. He was a galaxy of contradictions, a hall of mirrors. There were those who dismissed him as a sleazy opportunist, but his wife, Anna, was a respected author and had the bearing and style of a Hapsburg princess. Rupert himself was inscrutable. He did not flaunt his great power. Rather, he displayed a heavy calm, as if to dull his weighty presence.

For all that, he had an Australian irreverence for pomp and ceremony, and there was always a glint in his eye, some dangerous flicker of light, as if he could be measuring the distance between his fist and your jaw. It was just possible. He came out of nowhere, bought newspapers like hats, and if they were stodgy and hidebound and didn't suit him, he turned up the brim and showed you something different. He had the breathtaking courage of a pirate. Then he moved into television and the media trembled. The hotshot kids in executive denims knew in an instant that they were up against an even more dangerous killer.

At the Pierre dinner, moguls flirted with Rupert, who was on his best plutocrat behavior, and he walked past me, nodding, into their midst. Across the room, I saw Ian Rae, one of Rupert's "family," making odd motions with his arms. Rupert surrounded himself with such people—reliable, competent, worshipful, protective, and utterly loyal. He could order the man to burn down Paris and Ian would light the torch. These members of his "family" didn't work for money. They wanted to earn his approval. Members of the family wanted only to sun themselves in Rupert's singular light. And so when I saw Ian coming toward me, sweating, his eyes rolling with panic, I knew that he was acting for Rupert on some high purpose. He pulled me aside and in a hoarse whisper asked me why I wasn't on the plane.

"What plane?" I asked.

"The plane to Berlin," said an exasperated Rae. "What's wrong with you, mate? It's done. Finished. It's all coming apart."

"What? What's done? What's coming apart?"

"The Cold War! It's all over!"

"Come on!" I said. I could not think of any single act that would mark the unraveling of the vast, frozen Soviet empire.

"Tonight," he said, and I could tell that he was serious, because Ian didn't joke, especially not in a holy place like a gathering of important rich people. "They are tearing down the Berlin Wall!"

The East Germans, he explained, had come unglued. Even as we spoke, they were pouring through the checkpoints, making their own checkpoints, heading for the West. The East German guards were just standing by, grinning, allowing it to happen. It was a political miracle. The butchers in Europe were smiling!

Naturally, everybody with a press card and a passport was on his way to Berlin. It is a Pavlovian truth in this business: There are imperative moments and there are singular places, and now was the moment and Berlin was the place. Murdoch's people are instinctive men and they knew it in an instant. The Cold War was over!

Under Rupert's orders, Ian had chartered a jet for $100,000 to take a team from *A Current Affair* to Berlin. I was not so intoxicated with the story that I was not impressed by the sum. It seemed to me that we could get there for a lot less than $100,000. What about Rupert's private jet? I asked him. Wouldn't that be cheaper than a charter? He looked across the room where Rupert was chatting with some other moguls, then pulled himself together and made his way across the room and took Rupert aside. I could see Rupert listening, in that frowning, stormy silence of his, then uttering a few words to Ian, who came scampering back across the room.

"No, sorry," said Ian. "Rupert's got to use his plane. Going back to Australia for a funeral. You'll use the charter."

I suppose Rupert could still have given us the jet, but then he would have been forced to take a commercial flight to Sydney. Or maybe he was just signaling the urgency, the high importance of the event. You never knew with Rupert. No, better to give us the charter and make us understand that this one was without restraint. What was $100,000 compared to the end of the Cold War?

The troops were assembling at Fortune Garden, our out-of-office headquarters on Third Avenue. Get going, said Ian desperately. I, too, was seized with the overwhelming urgency of the moment, my head swimming with the romantic possibilities of the story, not to mention the effects of a few glasses of the bubbly. I went, tuxedo and all, cummerbund flying, happily chasing the biggest story of my life. Late, but not too late.

Luckily, I always carry a small bag with my passport and shaving gear. I jumped into a cab and headed for Fortune Garden. The restaurant was our new hangout—the Aussies always had to have a bar across the road from the office where they could conduct late business. The office wouldn't do, it was too restrictive. They couldn't drink there without feeling squeamish about violating professional ethics and experiencing some sense of sin. Not that they minded sin—sin was one of their favorite things—they just hadn't resolved it with the work ethic. They needed a bar to holler in, get wild and thrown out of, and they always commandeered one. It used to be The Racing Club on 67th Street, but someone pinched a waitress or hit a paying customer or otherwise crossed the line of rude behavior and we were temporarily mad at each other. Now it was Fortune Garden, and it always made me think of *A Thousand Clowns,* the scene where Murray Burns croons that anything can happen in a Chinese restaurant.

And so it was that night. When I got there, the bar was jammed with twenty-five excited producers, assistant producers, reporters, fetchers, researchers—and that peculiarly suppressed, fever-pitch flush of an exciting story. Waiters were bringing tray after tray of food. The bartender was opening beers as fast as he could, and he still couldn't keep up with that crowd. There is no tomorrow when you are on a big one.

Peter Brennan, our executive producer, had the place of honor at the bar and he was juggling three phones and two drinks at once: Lifting up the bottle, yelping at the phone, then chugging down the beer. He was drinking from the bottle because the Australians were convinced we poisoned our glasses with soap. Brennan was issuing orders, making demands, dispatching troops, and keeping himself poison-free from the bottle.

"Get some clothes!" he shouted to someone. "Get a crew. Get two crews!"

He was in fine form, lining it all up, the whole logistical and technical end of the industry flowing from the telephone console of that bar, heading for Berlin. All the teams and equipment had to be located, reserved, guaranteed. We were fighting against major networks, vast newspaper chains—the deepest deep-pockets of expense-account journalism were being mobilized and dispatched. Amid the cheerful chaos, assistant producers were running back and forth between the studio and the bar, pulling people off stories, away from assignments, interrupting lovemaking and fights—no one cared. Only the ones who were left out. I loved it.

Brennan looked up from his telephone console and his beer, saw me standing there, and grinned at me. He opened his arms and cried out, "Mate! Where've you been? Listen, we've got the hook."

He handed me a beer and barked into the phone that he didn't want to hear any excuses, none, just get it done, go, go, go! He punched another button and changed his tune, his voice sounding now like a sweet stiletto: "Oh, lovey, I know you can find some more cars!"

Then he put aside the phone and told me "the hook."

We were going to stage our own German reunification.

Brennan's daughter, Yasmin, was working as an assistant on the show. He had sent her out to comb the bars in the German Yorkville section of Manhattan with a specific purpose: find a thick, newly liberated ex-Commie who had links to the inclement gray interior of the Eastern bloc; find someone willing to return and be reunited with his family so that we could trail along and show the big picture in symbolic simplicity. We would use the sentimental story of this one reunification in tandem with touching, heart-wrenching sidebars running all the way from Teterboro Airport in New Jersey to the far East German frontiers on the shifting earth of Europe. It would be terrific, and the keepers of the flame—those members of the Fourth Estate who were convinced that television news had to build pyramids of parched facts to be pure—would hate it. Too bad for them.

Like everything else, however, it was easier said than done. Yasmin, it seemed, could not find an appropriately willing ex-Communist. She was going to all the bars in Yorkville and calling for hands for someone who had escaped from the East and wanted to be on television. They must have thought she was loony. Finally, someone at the Heidelberg on 86th Street took her seriously and said, "Ja! You want Luther."

"Who's Luther?"

East German, said the men at the bar.

"Where's Luther?"

You'll find him at Ryan's Daughter on 85th Street, they said. A bad sign. Luther could not find a German bar to celebrate the grandest night of post–World War II German history. He was toasting the new era and the end of the Berlin Wall in an Irish bar.

Someone could have detected an omen in that, but not us. We were on a mission.

Meanwhile Brennan sent me home for clothes. Everyone bring clothes and passports and money, he told the deploying troops, but this was *A Current Affair* and no one had much money. No matter how much we made, we were just a day short of payday—we thought it was glamorous. Nevertheless, we tapped all of our cash machines to the maximum and took collections from the assistant producers and the technicians— Brennan, sensing a certain hesitancy, had to grab the wallets and snarl that they'd get it all back. Because these kids knew us better than anyone, they made him sign chits.

When I had to ask my assistant, Amy, to drain her cash machine, I had to wonder why all these grown-ups running this show did not have a midnight source of money, and then I looked over at the bar where Brennan was pushing away the empties to make room for more beer, where young kids fresh out of college were trying to make the most intricate arrangements for the use of satellite time to feed back our stories, where overwhelmed Chinese waiters were trying to nail down food orders without insulting anyone by asking if they belonged to the outpatients from Fox Broadcasting, and I was ashamed that I could even raise such a silly topic. Of course, this would be done off the cuff, with that crude, unfinished quality that characterized our show. We were Rupert Murdoch's flying circus. The rough edges gave us our tone.

Finally, near one o'clock, Yasmin came in with our "hook." His name was Luther and he said that he was in construction. He was somewhere near fifty and he had a belly that bumped ahead of him, as well as that glazed, unsteady look of a man who had a head start in celebrating the freedom of his comrades. His head bobbed and weaved and his speech wandered along, trying to keep up.

Brennan sat him down, ordered coffee, and tried to see if we were linking our fate to a madman. Luther looked at Brennan, then leaned over past the coffee and took one of the bottles of beer. Yes, yes, said Luther, he knew all about East Germany. He had a brother, a comrade, one of the bosses. I could see the reunion blooming in Brennan's eyes. The structure was there, even if the instrument—Luther—was a little shaky. There was one more important question: Did Luther have a passport?

Of course he had a passport. Luther traveled back and forth to Europe all the time. When Luther said that, something began to tickle my suspicious system. A man in construction who made regular trips to Europe? No, no, now was not the time to get too inquisitive. We needed Luther. We didn't want to see something that would kill the hook.

Where was the passport? asked Brennan. Back in his apartment in the Bronx, said Luther. He lived with a fourth or fifth cousin. Luther offered to go get it, but Brennan was too shrewd for that. He had sized up his man and decided that was not a man you allowed out of your sight. So he sent Yasmin to Luther's home with a note, and to make doubly certain, Luther called the house and alerted the distant cousin that Yasmin was coming. It was a little unsettling that the fourth cousin was not in the least surprised at the arrangement.

Meanwhile private cabs began to form a line up on Third Avenue. Into them with their plush leather seats we packed cases of equipment, metal containers of videotapes, boxes of cameras, editing machines, lights—and, at the last minute, like some impish beast, Gordon Elliott, our six-foot-seven, three-hundred-and-thirty-pound gorilla. He was supposed to have his wedding party the next day, but when Brennan called, Gordon didn't hesitate. He told his bride that he was going to Berlin. She could go ahead and have the wedding party without him. Duty, and all that.

"My mistake," he would tell me later, in a rare moment of sober, reflective candor, "was that I was so happy about the assignment. I couldn't help smiling. It made the bride very mad. Yes, that was where I made my mistake."

Also with us was David Lee Miller, our own, personal

neurotic. Miller is a cross between Richard Benjamin and Woody Allen. His only fear is not being liked. Or missing a story. Or getting scooped. Or not finishing his vegetables. Or his mother calling him in Berlin. This will tell you everything about David: He was in the midst of a long-standing relationship with a lawyer when he worked in Cleveland. When he lost his job and came to New York, she came to visit. Let us call her Adrian, because that's her name. The minute she stepped off the plane, David was dispatched to Alaska to run down a story about UFOs. Someone else might have begged off, but not David. He was too terrified that he might never again get the call. Nevertheless, the relationship survived. They cared for each other. David promised Adrian that he would make up for it when they took a joint vacation in California. You have to picture it: It is Friday evening and they are walking on the beach in Malibu on a sweet summer evening. David is carrying his cellular phone. It begins to beep and he answers it—he answers it! It is Peter Brennan on the line. David has to catch a plane back to New York to cover a story, and not even a whole story—to back up another reporter who is covering a story. Sunday morning. Be there! "I'll be there," David vows to the phone. He gazes down at the woman we'll call Adrian and she glares back with a look of such passion that it made David shiver. "I have never seen such hate," he told me. He tries to mollify her. He pleads. "We still have all of Saturday," he tells Adrian.

He never sees her again.

That's the kind of people we assembled to go to Berlin—people who carried cellular phones on the beach, people who were happy to skip their own wedding party.

* * *

I had to call my wife. This was not an ordinary late-excuse call about the press of business: "Honey, I'll be a little late for dinner so you go ahead and eat; I'll just pick up something in Berlin." This was cold revenge. As most people know, I am married to Connie Chung of CBS News—not exactly a vegetating housewife. Just a few hours earlier, I discovered, she had left a message on our answering machine saying that *she* would not be home for dinner because she would be anchoring the Berlin coverage from 57th Street. She was always leaving me these little bombshells, saying that she'd be late or back in a few days because she was going to Israel to cover a story, or to Los Angeles to interview Jane Fonda.

On some ordinary night it was a little depressing to come home and find her loving voice announcing that instead of that planned cozy dinner of takeout Chinese food, she was off to Pakistan to interview the new President, or racing to China to record a seismic shift of power. Some exotic clime or dramatic doing always tugging at her sleeve for attention.

In professional terms, Connie was hot, and for a long time I had been plain Mister Chung to the doormen in our apartment building. With *A Current Affair,* however, things had turned around. For one thing, the mailman now knew my name. So I was Mister Cool when I called her at the studio on the car phone. I let her go on and on—she was very apologetic and said she was sorry, but she was going to be swamped with the story for the next few days and we probably wouldn't be able to get together for a while. I said, with saintlike understanding: "Oh, yeah, I got your message. That's okay, honey, I won't be home either."

"Oh, really, why not?" I could hear her eyebrows arch.

"Well, sweetheart, I gotta cover a story. I'll be in Berlin. You know how it is."

There are moments in that domestic tussle of egos called marriage when such satisfaction is not only permissible, but required. How sweet! How delicious! How childish!

I was still smiling when we got to Teterboro Airport in New Jersey, where the monster $100,000 chartered G-2 Gulfstream was waiting. Field producer Nancy Gershwin was not smiling, however. The grand-niece of George Gershwin was fretting. We were unprepared, and many of us were drunk. She was also very angry because she had just come back from Germany that afternoon. Didn't even unpack. She'd done a piece on Hitler's secretary, and Brennan had found her at the airport and just turned her around. She was dead tired, pissed, loaded down with smelly luggage, and now on her way back to the same Germany from which she'd just come. But we needed her. She spoke German and knew how things worked in Berlin. You needed hardheaded people who knew the way of things. God knows there were few enough of them in our ragged and soggy group.

Gordon Elliott, a man of some proportions as well as someone who always spotted and seized the main chance, immediately passed out on the nine-foot couch. It was impressive that they had a couch that would accommodate a man of his size, but this was an impressive aircraft. They had desks, chairs, typewriters, and telephones in the sky. They also had an open bar—just what we needed.

As cloudy and irresponsible as I can be, I have moments of bright and complete lucidity. Something told me that I had better get something down on tape before we all settled into a drunken coma. It's an old newshound's trick: get something in the can in case you have a meltdown. At least you'll have something to show on the air. I looked over at Luther. With his hair slack across his sweating skull and his sore, unsteady eyes, he seemed to be making odd noises of regret about what he'd gotten himself into. I would have to interview Luther before it was too late, but I wasn't looking forward to it. You get that kind of feeling when a man tries to avert his face from the camera, as if he might be recognized and arrested the minute we landed. There was something hidden about Luther, something he wasn't telling us.

Nevertheless we organized one crew, Dick and Teresa Fisher, and I sat across from Luther by the window so the viewers would know that we were on a plane, en route to an historic rendezvous, with the sound of the engines in the rear adding to the drama, and I began to ask questions.

"How long has it been since you've seen your brother, Helmut?" I asked Luther. I thought, maybe eight, nine years; at least before *glasnost*, long before the hope of *perestroika*. A time when separations were tragic and final. In any case I was trying to provoke some tender memories, rouse Luther from his torpor, and revive the serious purpose and deeper meaning of our trip. How long, Luther?

"Mumble, mumble, mumble."

I didn't hear that. The jet engines, no doubt. I asked it again. "How long, Luther, since you've laid eyes on your brother, Helmut?"

In an all-too-audible voice I heard Luther's reply. "About a year," he said.

Wait a minute. You left East Germany three decades ago. Yes, yes, true, he admitted, but it seemed that Luther had business interests that took him back and forth to Berlin and that he visited the East on a more or less regular basis.

Business interests! What business interests? You're supposed to be a construction worker, for Christ's sake!

Luther shifted in his seat and rolled his head around and said in his nonspecific way that his main occupation was construction—this was perfectly true—but that he had a few sidelines. Nothing much. Just to put some bread on the table. A man is entitled to a few sidelines, he said with a show of indignation.

Burt Kearns, our managing editor, was shaking his head. Nancy Gershwin was ready to kill. I was somewhere between amused and enraged. This was supposed to be an historic, heart-wrenching reunion. How can you be historic after only a year? We were off on a million-dollar spree with a world-class adventurer.

Never mind. We were pros. We could handle it.

"You must be real anxious to see your brother, now that the Wall is coming down and East is meeting West."

Luther was silent. And nervous.

"Right? I mean, you do have a brother in the East."

"Oh, yes. Helmut. My brother. Of course I have a brother. Ha, ha."

"You must be anxious to see him."

Luther fidgeted. You get to know the way someone fidgets during an interview whether or not they're being even minimally candid. After years of interviewing liars and obfuscators, you can detect a nervous, evading fidgeter. And Luther was definitely sitting on something.

"And your brother will be glad to see you."

Well, maybe he would not be so happy, Luther said, because, well, Helmut was a dedicated member of the Communist Party, and he was the foreman of a die plant, an important member of the industrial ruling class. And as he turned and twisted in his seat, his eyes roving, Luther conceded that he and his brother had a somewhat troubled relationship. In fact, his last visit had ended when Helmut had kicked Luther out of his house.

Kearns and Gershwin were grinding their teeth, probably

drowning out the engine noise, but we were committed and we taped an interview. Luther was a lamb, a nice member of the working class, a construction worker who was going to be reunited with his long-lost brother on *A Current Affair*, whether he liked it or not.

By the time we landed in England everyone was cold sober, shivering in the sudden winter of November in Europe. The crew of the chartered jet bailed out. They were only going as far as England, then they were bringing the jet back to America for another charter. They looked, somehow, relieved.

We were transferring equipment to two smaller jets which would carry us to Berlin, trying to outthink our mistakes. "Mate, this is the way to travel," said Gordon Elliott, slapping me on the back with entirely too much gusto. The sheer adventure had caught his imagination. I did not remind him that his wedding party in New York would soon be getting underway. In any case, it wouldn't disturb him that he wouldn't be there for it. He was after the wild thing, chasing the flutter of a big chance that always seemed to captivate these Australians. They were untroubled gamblers, creatures of impulse, set off like puppies after a moving object.

Luther had another suggestion. He wanted to stay in England. We could put him up at a hotel, and he could come when we found his brother and "set it all up." He began to look a little frightened. He didn't understand. There is one rule about television. You have got to show up. You can be untalented, unkempt, unshaved, wrinkled and incoherent—but you've got to show up. Now he was looking down the barrel of Burt Kearns' loaded eye. Kearns was not gonna let Luther out. Not alive.

Burt Kearns could be a hard guy. You're going, he said to

25

Luther, and Luther, who had grown up under the unblinking
cement watchtowers of the hardest of hard-liners, knew that he
was trapped. He'd have to tunnel out of Kearns' grasp. Of
course by now everyone was a little testy. Hangover tempers
on hair triggers; not a pretty sight. Luther saw that we would
roll over him like a panzer division if he balked, and he
shrugged and became one of us. Not that we ever took our eyes
off of him for a minute.

Meanwhile we were joined by another crew—a British cameraman and a soundman hired long-distance by Brennan from
the bar at Fortune Garden. And they looked it. Sleepy free-
lancers who didn't give a shit about the story or us, but were
working per diem, on the clock, and clicking off the time like
a taxi meter. They would aim the camera and the microphone
where they were told to, but don't expect much more.

Not the rest of us. We were enthusiasts. The plane had
hardly stopped rolling when assistants were on the phone,
trying to arrange for cars to meet us at the airport in Berlin.
Someone else was handing out wire copies of news updates.
We all felt that particular lump in the throat that came from
being so far away from the scene of the action. We were
reporters, soldiers, and we marched to the sound of the guns.
There was something terrible about the fear of missing a story.
Even when you're in close touch, there is a small voice of panic
that whispers, "You are too late. They will all be going home
just when you arrive. You screwed it up again, like you have
screwed up before in your long, bumpy past." It is a newshound's anthem. When they handed me fresh bulletins, with
short, clipped paragraphs singing the story of the Iron Curtain
meltdown, it felt even worse. I should be there now. Furthermore, we'd left New York late at night and flown into the
clock. It was now eleven in the morning and we had to be on

the air at four in the afternoon. It was nerve-racking to cut it so fine.

I don't even remember the flight to Berlin, except that when we hit the runway, we hit it running. The air was electric as people poured out of the planes and spoke in a rush—couldn't get the words out fast enough. We forged ahead, late, but in Berlin at last. It was just past noon.

The overwhelming mood was happy confusion. There were no reservations at the hotel and it didn't matter. Burt sent off killer assistants with no-excuses orders to get the rooms. It was like a desperate battle: Don't come back alive if you fail. There were two small cars waiting for us at the airport and we grabbed more. Burt told an assistant, "Hire the first six cars in the cab line."

"For how long?"

"Forever! Indefinitely!"

Loaded down with cars and equipment and that engine of fear because we are late, we marched on the city. Listen, I told Kearns, I'll do a few stand-ups. One at the Brandenburg Gate, one at Checkpoint Charlie. Just to show the flag. Get that back to New York and establish that we have territorial claims to the story. Gordon Elliott, meanwhile, wanted to get to the Brandenburg Gate. What he would do when he got there was anybody's guess.

By chance, Gordon plucked one young cabdriver who spoke English. His name was Yves, and he came from one of those hybrid European aristocracies: plenty of money, yet with a feel for the back streets and black markets. Yves was a willing co-conspirator who was in it for the thrill of the chase. What a perfect match. Gordon and Yves. As expected, Gordon told him to find the biggest BMW in Berlin. That took Yves about ten minutes to accomplish.

David Lee Miller had a more conventional idea, but an evergreen when it came to such a story. He would take some newly liberated East Germans shopping. After all, isn't that what this was all about, the contest between materialism and dialectics? Show them the goods that they had been denied in their gray, sterile world. Watch their eyes pop. So he went off in a car to find some shoppers. David tends to be a little antsy, so it was better to let him go off in search of a story, allowing his natural talents to flower. There was also that other consideration. If we let him hang around he'd drive everyone nuts.

All in all we were not in bad shape. Of course someone had to find the microwave truck coming down from Hamburg. Without the microwave we could not hit the satellite. In addition, we had the satellite only for a little while because we were renting time and only so much was available. Networks could hog great chunks of time, but we weren't a big network. Don't worry, mate, said Brennan back in New York, everything's fine. And, oh, by the way, you have to get on the satellite an hour early—at three in the afternoon. It was already twelve-thirty. We scattered like mice to find something to put on the air.

It was bedlam at the Brandenburg Gate. It was not just the size of the crowds, although the press of flesh was unimaginable; there were people everywhere. What was so impressive was the stifled emotion. The people gathered in that place were choked with all the years of unexpressed suffering. All the pain of that damned Wall was felt by everyone. They'd all seen the bodies sprawled across the razor wire. They all knew someone who'd died trying to break through. There was a restless expectation, as if we would see some raw evidence of what was taking place, some moment of high drama that would express it, make it concrete. The people were roused and awakened, but unable to comprehend what was taking place. A great, historical moment was passing unheralded except by default.

Someone handed me something to eat, but I couldn't even swallow because of the scene before my eyes. All up and down the border, the Wall itself was alive with kids. Flower children, like in the sixties. They all looked brave and innocent and just short of bawling with pride. They were sitting or standing on top of the Berlin Wall—an act that days earlier would have cost them their lives—grinning. Some of them were clapping or singing or hugging each other. But mostly, they were just grinning. Their legs dangled over the sides of the Wall as if they were swimmers testing the temperature of the water. For so many years it had been this cruel block of dead cement. Now it was alive.

It was a strange revolution. The people who came across from the East were visiting another star system. And we were ready for them—the media. I stood there in my blue sweater and my microphone, and I looked up and there was Peter Jennings, standing like a conquering hero on top of a truck. On my right, way up in the air, Dan Rather stood inside the bucket of a giant crane. Tom Brokaw was the subtle Napoleon, strolling amongst the crowd, accepting the tributes that were his due because he had been here a day earlier and broken the story, and the rest of us would never catch up to that coup.

It was twelve forty-five, we were outgunned and outmanned, but I didn't care. We had 189 markets and 25 million viewers, I had covered everything from Watergate to the Middle East, and this was good enough for me. I was going on the air from Berlin with the end of the Cold War!

Chapter
Two

MEANWHILE, though, there was that little matter of our "hook" to take care of—the touching reunion.

I was talking to New York on a pretty regular basis, and Brennan had developed that unsettling and insufferable calm adopted by people who are in control—like doctors soothing bleeders.

"How's Luther?" he asked.

"Oh, Luther's fine," I lied.

"We're using him in all the promotions. Him and his brother."

Great. An advertising blitz dedicated to a dubious defector and a bigshot Commie brother one hundred miles deep in the East German hinterland. Only those of us who had gotten close enough to Luther to sense the deep pocket of trouble knew the chance we were taking.

And so, while I stayed in West Berlin doing the harder news stories, Burt Kearns and his hearty band plunged into Red Germany in search of a sentimental sidelight to the busting of the borders. Burt Kearns took the BMW, a car which would impress the local cops and give some stamp of authority to the group on the sojourn, and he took our hired German cabdriver, Yves, who could bluff the bureaucrats they might encounter along the way. He also took the English crew with their woeful, smug indifference.

And then he tried to take Luther. Only Luther wasn't going. He dug in his heels and said that for good and sufficient reasons he refused to venture into the East. I could easily believe that he had good and sufficient reasons—but it was my job to make this thing work. So I took Luther and Kearns for a walk.

"Why won't you go?" I asked Luther.

"Because I have no visa," he said.

Kearns was blistering mad. "You've got a West German passport," he said. "That's good enough. They won't bother you."

Luther shook his head. "No," he said. "You people have American passports; they won't bother you. American passports still count for a lot in the world." Furthermore, he pointed out, "you have press credentials, which practically makes you immune from all authority." Besides—and he was much more emphatic about this now—his brother would not see him anyway. It was all a big mistake. He had been crazy with drink when he agreed to the deal; he was sorry for all the trouble and inconvenience and we could send him a bill for the airfare and the food.

Kearns looked grim. His jaw was set and his feet were planted and I could sense that rising bubble of stubborn will begin to assert itself. "What does your brother like?" he asked Luther.

Luther did not understand the question.

Kearns almost snarled. "What does he like? Nylons? American chocolate? Chewing gum? What hard goods does he need?"

This Luther understood. Now we were talking business, not airy concepts. "Bananas," said Luther. "Everyone in East Germany likes bananas."

Kearns thought he heard wrong. "Bananas?"

"You cannot get bananas in the East," said Luther. "Impossible."

And so Kearns sent Yves and the English crew and anyone else he could lay hands on out to corner the West Berlin banana market. Like everything else, they were good at it. In no time at all, Kearns was the West German banana king. You never saw so many. He could have opened a jungle. First Kearns put Luther into the BMW and made him lie on the floor of the car. The bananas were piled on top. The trunk was loaded with them. Even the glove compartment had a few unripe, green bananas stuffed in with the maps. This is how we will go, he told Luther. No one will see you. All they will see are the bananas.

"But what if we're stopped?" asked Luther. "We could be stopped."

"If we are stopped, you are our hostage. You never saw us before. We snatched you off a West Berlin street, forced you into the car under duress, and piled all these bananas on top of you. We are banana smugglers and we told you that you had to take us to East Germany or else."

Luther saw what I saw: Kearns had been driven insane and would do anything for the story. Luther was, indeed, his hostage and had no choice but to lead him into East Germany with this heap of bananas. And so off they went, up to their automatic windows and radiophone in tropical fruit.

It turned out to be a great quest. Luther got Kearns and the crew blindly lost. You can't blame him entirely; it's hard to navigate when you're hiding under bunches of bananas on the floor of the car. You can't see the road. Nonetheless, Kearns was lost and worried about losing his natural light. Unlike the stand-ups at the Brandenburg Gate, where darkness cast the joyful story in a sorrowful, almost melancholy counterpoint, daylight would work for the reunion, purify this semistaged event. Kearns knew that it was our major story for the Monday show. He knew that we had been promoting it. Brennan had put it on the air and there had been ads in the newspapers about this heart-wrenching scene that had yet to take place.

Kearns did the only thing that he could do while waiting for the roads and maps to match: he told the British crew to shoot as much background and scenery as possible. Get the rolling countryside, the cows. He even dug Luther out of his banana pit and sat him up and had him gaze out the window as if he were looking forward to a reunion. Luther only managed to look like he was awaiting the gallows. Once or twice, as they were passing through some quaint village square, they were stopped by the police. Yves leaned his head out the window and smiled his charming smile and said the magic words: American television. Then he handed out bananas and they were ushered deeper and deeper into East Germany, slipping on the urgent banana peel of our deadline.

Meanwhile, the English crew was as usual completely at ease. Whenever Burt inquired about the state of the running shots, the cameraman would reply in a voice of boredom and utter lack of concern, "Don't worry, luv, we got you covered."

Such confidence! Such utter sangfroid! Such idiots!

No fool, Kearns worried. That is one of the job require-
ments for a field producer: worry. Intense, wall-to-wall worry.
Shoot tape, he told them. Shoot the countryside. Shoot the
villages. Get the church steeples. They aimed at the fields and
the trees and the road signs and the curious natives giving them
curious looks, and Kearns began to think that he was covering
his ass. Every once in a while Luther poked up his head and
asked where they were, and Kearns lied and said almost there.
Poor Luther was terrified that the secret police were going to
pull them over and drag him out from under the bananas and
have a summary execution.

Finally, after driving for hours, after examining maps and
road signs like troop commanders, they found the die plant
where Helmut worked. The hard part was over, thought
Kearns. "Where is your brother's house?" he asked, pulling
Luther out from under his banana cave. Luther blinked, looked
around, and said that he had no idea. Somehow it all looked
strange. Kearns slapped his own head. The English crew
smiled at each other, enjoying the misery. Yves found the town
square and a tavern where he made inquiries. Someone pointed
to a house near the end of town, and Luther turned pale. A
cynic could almost believe that he really didn't want to find his
brother's house.

They drove up to the house and the crew hung back a little,
catching the moment on tape. Kearns hit the clapper on the
door, but no one answered. He banged louder, but still no one
answered. He could hear movement behind the door, see cur-
tains stir, and then clamp shut, but no one came to the door.
Finally Kearns began to pound—really hammer away—at the
door, and began to scream and threaten to break it down.
Helmut's wife unbolted the locks, opened the door a crack, and

Kearns and Yves pleaded and begged to see Helmut. His wife looked up and saw Luther standing sheepishly in the rear of the group and screamed and slammed the door. They could hear the bolts being shot home.

Luther smiled at Kearns and shrugged.

The British crew told Kearns not to worry, they'd got all that dramatic shit on tape. Kearns did not know whom to kill. Yves, meanwhile, was pleading pathetically through the closed door, saying that lives and careers hung in the balance. Children could go hungry unless Helmut spent a moment beside his brother. What would it cost? A tiny moment. They could hear the rumble of loud voices and make out a word or two and, finally, bending to the tug of the media or pity for the children who would go hungry, Helmut opened the door.

His wife stood between Helmut and Luther, and when the two brothers looked at each other there was fire in their eyes, but I suppose by the broadest and most generous possible interpretation, one could say that, technically, a reunion did take place. Not that an impartial witness looking at it would ever believe that anyone in that group liked each other—thank God for Helmut's wife acting as a demilitarized zone. Whatever grudge lay between these brothers, Kearns did not want to know. He got his shots, and he stood offstage crossing his fingers, closing his eyes in prayer, hoping for the brothers to embrace, put their arms around each other. They moved like men prodded at the point of a bayonet and seemed to put their arms around each other. Helmut's wife was still between them, however, a guarantee against bloodshed. In the annals of reunions, there have been gentler ones in hell.

Nevertheless, we had Brennan's hook. Kearns even got it in daylight. At least he had enough daylight and enough reunion to justify the promotions. Naturally, he wanted to murder

Luther, but unfortunately he didn't have enough time. They had to get back to Berlin and edit and transmit. There was a tense moment of goodbye. No one quite knew how to conduct it. Of course it was a relief for everyone, but there was always that temptation to say the one thing that would set off a melee.

Kearns did not let it get that far. He shoved Luther back into the car, left a generous supply of bananas, and yelled a hearty farewell. Then he ordered the driver to race back to Berlin, and off they went, hitting 65, 75, 85 miles an hour, tossing out bananas to cops and bystanders—anyone who they happened to pass. By the time they got to Berlin, they were out of bananas, and Luther had somewhat recovered. Somehow they had gotten through the worst of it, and now he could relax, order drinks, and find some trouble.

We had managed to bag a dozen hotel rooms, one of which was converted into an editing room. Kearns was strutting through the hotel, pleased with himself about his great coup in getting a reunion, when Gordon Elliott came out of the editing room and said, "Too bad about the tape."

There was a moment when everyone's mouth hung open. Gordon must be joking. What could he be joking about? Surely not the Luther material. Not even Gordon Elliott, master of a million pranks, would joke about the sacred subject. Then the faces moved again and Kearns ran into the editing room where he found Teresa Fisher, our editor, with her head in her hands, weeping like a child. She showed Kearns the raw footage, which consisted of blank tape. The English crew had screwed it up. Kearns staggered out of the room and tracked down the English crew, who were sipping beers and in their usual state of indifference.

"What happened?" he shouted. "Where's the countryside? Where's the quaint Bavarian villages? Where's Luther in the

37

window of the car, waiting for the dramatic reunion with his beloved brother? What the hell happened?"

"We were just talking about that," said the cameraman.

The possibilities were endless. Bad exposure. Bad battery. Bad tape. Any number of things could have gone wrong.

"Happens like that sometimes," said the soundman with a shrug.

Kearns did not hesitate. He turned to Teresa and said, "We're going back." He turned to Luther and said, "You too." At which point Luther screamed and fled into the street. Kearns sent a hulking Gordon after him, and when Gordon brought him back, Luther was grim and pale. Kearns looked at him. "You're going back," he said the way MacArthur promised to return to the Philippines. Nothing was going to stop him from getting this story, no matter how ugly it got.

But it never came to that. Using some technical tricks, Teresa was able to salvage some of the so-called reunion. The stuff they shot inside the house using strobe lighting was recognizable. The tape looked washed out and amateurish, but everyone was there being reunited. The best part was that no one would have to go back. This seemed to help Luther's respiration, which had stopped.

But we weren't done yet.

NATO and the Warsaw Pact were puny and toothless threats compared to what we were about to unleash upon the unsuspecting civilians of East and West Berlin.

Gordon Elliott had been roaming around the city looking for ideas, and he had just come back from the Brandenburg Gate. "There are these great crowds, right, mate? They're all gathered up, expecting a show, only there's no show. There are only people milling about. I tell you, mate, we are going to give them a show."

He does not make idle threats. Gordon had seen a few of the West Germans chipping away at the wall with little hammers, and while he admired the sentiment, he thought that the scale was all wrong. These people were whittling little arrowheads and he wanted to knock the damn thing down. And so he tried to find a pickax in the hotel to launch a full-scale attack on the Berlin Wall. Management thought he should leave the fire axes alone in case there was a fire. They called security in case Gordon didn't appreciate their point and decided to take matters in his own hands.

"Never mind, mate," said the indomitable Elliott. He left the hotel and searched out a nearby hardware store. They had axes, but they were anemic little things designed to chop up firewood or make toothpicks. He wanted something big, substantial. You know, to knock down a wall. Maybe a pick. The owner of the hardware store, already wary of this Goliath, shook his head. No ax. No pick. Gordon was momentarily stumped, but still determined. Where would I find a pickax? he asked himself.

Of course! The Fire Department!

It happened that there was a fire station near the Wall. With good reason. Most of their calls were for burning cars, shot up by the East German police during escape attempts. The firemen—great big guys themselves—had a natural affinity for a king-sized reporter like Gordon. Sure they had a pick, what kind of firemen do you think we have in Berlin? Unfortunately, they claimed that they needed it, you know, in case of a fire. Gordon explained that he just wanted to borrow it, but the firemen were stubborn and said that they needed their ax for their work. Gordon would not be denied. He took out a wad of Deutschemarks and started to peel off very large bills.

The firemen went into a huddle and emerged agreeing that while they could not in all conscience sell Gordon their ax, since it was the property of the West Berlin municipality and selling it would be a clear violation of the rules, they could not see anything wrong with renting it to him. Of course, if he saw or heard about a fire, he had to bring it back. But they'd rent it to him at the rate of, say, the equivalent of $100 an hour. Great, said Gordon, handing over $200 worth of Deutschemarks. "I'll take it for two hours."

It was dark and the people were still nibbling at the Wall when Gordon got there with his pickax. Instantly, they recognized him for what he was—a provocateur of the media art. A Western journalist with a pickax and his own film crew. A cheer went up from the frustrated masses at the Wall. Gordon rose to the occasion, climbing the Wall and making a passionate speech denouncing foul Communism, humorless Marxism, dull dialectics, and boring bureaucracy. The crowd responded, and Gordon could see that he was right. He provided the missing ingredient in the great spectacle: a show. He was like some unfettered bull elephant calling to his herd in the night. It hardly mattered that the people below probably did not understand his odd mixture of Liverpool and Sydney Cockney. They were crazy with the spunk and spirit of this madman atop the Berlin Wall waving a fireman's pickax like a baton. He stood astride the Wall, silhouetted in the night, his arms spread out like some political and social rock star, crying a primitive version of freedom—and that was something that they all understood.

Then, with his coat flying in the wind and his cries echoing over the crowd, he took one great whack at the Wall with his pickax. It could have been Paul Bunyan up there, so great was the impact on the Wall and on the crowd. It was what they had been waiting for—the dismantling of that hated symbol. Again and again Gordon sunk the point of his pick into the frozen stone, and each time he struck it, he hit a nerve among the suddenly united people of East and West Berlin. Some howled. Some cheered. And some wept.

Finally, after all that piddling stuff with the little hammers, great cracks appeared in the Wall. It would come down after all. The tape crew below caught him in all his glory, his face beaming, his coat flying, the pickax breaking up the Cold War itself.

And then, almost naturally, as if this was the way it was supposed to be and they all sensed it, a man climbed up and asked Gordon for the ax so that he could claim his fair share of that event. He too wanted a swipe at the Wall. And Gordon, being the generous creature that he was, handed him the pickax and stepped aside. Bulbs flickered in the night as world-class photojournalists recognized by instinct an authentic moment that ought to be captured on film.

So it was that the man next to Gordon Elliott, the man to whom he handed his pickax, became the cover photo of *Newsweek*. It would have been lovely—and maybe even more poetically correct—if they had used a picture of Gordon Elliott on the cover of the newsmagazine, but they picked the next guy in line.

Not that he was unhappy with himself. Gordon was bubbling with fresh ideas. He couldn't get over the contrast between the two sides of the border. These poor people had been deprived of sensual delights by their rigid oppressors, and he was just the man to introduce them to sin. And so he did a segment of a show on what I would call "A Walk on the Wild Side." Gordon escorted a sedate East German group through the X-rated section of West Berlin. He took them to topless bars, sex shops where they displayed strange implements of a carnal nature—devices so foreign and bizarre that the East Germans were confused and baffled about exactly what they were used for. He walked them past the red-light prostitutes who were crooning invitations at the country bumpkins. So innocent were these East Berliners that they could not tell the difference between the hookers and the transvestites.

I asked Gordon, "Is this why we fought the Cold War? To share the fleshpots of the world?"

"Damn right," he replied without hesitation.

David Lee Miller found his shoppers. They were students, a twenty-one-year-old boy and a twenty-year-old girl. David took them to the swankest department store in Berlin and, as he suspected, their eyes glazed over at the abundance.

He took the guy into the electronics section and the kid's eyes misted over. I know it's just things, but watching him run his hands over the smooth, new items, I realized that over a period of time the deprivation of goods, the unrealized yearning for things, sinks down and disables that part of us that is very close to hope. He bought the kid a stereo. David asked him to open it and take a look at it, because he wanted to show the reaction on television. But the kid refused. He wouldn't do it. There was something too private about such naked emotion. He was moved beyond words, beyond our comprehension, and he wanted to savor the moment alone. We had to respect that.

It wasn't just a game show, after all.

The girl was redheaded and had a glint of something devilish in her eye. David asked her what she wanted and she said that she wanted a denim jacket. She was already wearing a denim jacket, but she wanted another one. David, being the smart cookie that he was, agreed to the jacket, but asked her to do him a favor. He just wanted her to try on an evening gown. She couldn't refuse.

He took her to the formal-wear department and the saleswomen went nuts. They were like girls playing with a doll, fitting her with this dress and that accessory. Finally they found the ideal outfit. They fitted her with a slinky, black-beaded gown. You could hear the salesgirls sighing in the background as she walked across the floor—this redheaded knockout from East Germany. She smiled in a sly, secret sort of way, the way that Greta Garbo smiled in *Ninotchka* when she wore silk.

But she only wanted the denim jacket, no doubt on practical grounds. There weren't many places to wear slinky gowns in the East yet.

At the end of the day the students crossed back into the East, the boy with his unpacked stereo tucked under his arm and the girl with her twin denim jacket under hers, and it was time for me to leave as well. My last sight of Berlin was yet another Gordon Elliott memento.

People were beginning to know Gordon in West Berlin. Merchants refused to deal with him. He wanted to commit one last defiant gesture before we left, however, and he went back to his hardware store and asked for the spray paint section. The manager was standing before a ninety-foot display of spray paint, but he spread himself out in front of it, trying to shield it from Gordon, and said that his store didn't carry spray paint cans. He knew a troublemaker when he saw one.

Gordon found another store with another display of cans.

This time he didn't ask. He went straight to the display and took his cans, then marched to the counter and paid. He went back to the Wall, where he painted the *Current Affair* logo— the orange pyramid and the blue letters. The residents didn't understand it, but they knew it was unauthorized and they saw it was gorgeous. For a little while all that stood between Communism and Capitalism was Gordon Elliott and his painted pyramid. Kilroy had been there!

And all of it, from Luther's reunion to Gordon's pickax and spray paint, was showing up in the homes of 20 million Americans.

It was just another day in the life.

Chapter
Three

I grew up lighter than air. It was a trick taught to me by my father, who had somehow cracked America's greatest secret. The secret was confidence. Act bold, my father said when I was young and impressionable and actually listened to such advice. Just behave as if you belong and no one will challenge your presence—you will be able to go where you want to go.

This lesson did not come free of charge for my father, whose given name was Shirley—a name not uncommon for males in New England, where he had been born just after the turn of the century. To bear such a name he had to develop a resolute and sturdy character that served him well throughout life. (I had my own share of heartache in those emotionally tender school years when cold-blooded kids, learning his name, would invariably ask me if my mother's name was George.)

As a matter of fact, my father's brazen tactic worked. Not

once during my entire youth in my own hometown of Washington, D.C., did I ever have to use a ticket to get into Griffith Stadium to see the Washington Senators play baseball. I just marched through the ballpark gate showing only my plucky smile; the attendants would nod and let me pass unmolested through the turnstile, as if I really belonged.

Of course it helped that Shirley Povich was the respected, not to mention all-powerful, sports editor and columnist for the *Washington Post*. I could get into ball games, training camps, locker rooms—anything. When I was eight I was made a clubhouse boy for the Washington Senators. It was a lowly job, but I got to see the legends returning from WW II: Early Wynn, Bob Feller, Ted Williams, Joe DiMaggio, Stan Musial.

At the end of every winter we moved to Orlando, Florida, for spring training. We'd rent a house or apartment for a month or two. Until my parents found out how terrible the schools were, I would go to school locally, and in the afternoons get a job with the team because of my dad. In 1948 I traveled to St. Petersburg, where the Yankees trained, during that last winter of Babe Ruth's life. I met him, and although it was very warm, he was wearing a camel's hair coat because he was so sick. He smiled at me. As long as I live, there'll never be such moments. DiMaggio. Ted Williams. Babe Ruth!

When you hang around them, you call them by their first names. It was Joe and Ted and Stan, and I was Shirley's kid, Maury. "Hey, Shirley's kid, get me a Dr Pepper! Get me a towel! Clean my shoes!"

The next year I was the ball boy, and then I became the batboy, which was a grand position. I could boss the ball boy and the clubhouse boy. The pecking order was in my favor now.

When they made me batboy, I was ten and not quite ready to handle it. My mother was sitting with the venerable old owner of the Senators, Clark Griffith, who was well into his eighties at the time. We were at Tinker Field in Orlando, and I was so mesmerized by the action that I stood at home plate and watched this giant major leaguer slide into the plate. He tumbled into me and I went one way and the bat went the other and the player gave me a look of great scorn. Griffith turned to my mother and said, "Ethyl, your son is going to get killed if he doesn't learn what to do."

I didn't care. I had confidence, just like my dad taught me. This public nonchalance was how I would eventually come to work in television. I became a breezy character with a public composure that I can only describe as lighter-than-air. But now I stay out of the way of home plate.

Confidence, in fact, was what I tried to display on that June morning in 1986 when I boarded the commuter shuttle to New York, summoned urgently for a meeting by my new boss, Australian media baron Rupert Murdoch. Confidently and carefully I folded my suit jacket so that it wouldn't wrinkle. It was the gray jacket; gray was the absolute right choice. I had come to this conclusion during the sleepless night when I had weighed pinstripes against plaid, a blazer against a suit. The gray would appear jaunty as well as nicely confident. After all, the man wasn't going to fire me, was he?

No, he was going to pat me on the back and praise my work as host of *Panorama,* the daytime show on his freshly acquired Washington station. He was going to tell me what a swell job I'd been doing anchoring the prime-time newscast, too.

Or else he was going to fire me.

In 1985 Murdoch had bought the Washington station where I was happy as a clam working the daytime talk show and anchoring the late news. With me there always had to be some news connection. *Panorama,* with its celebrity guests, cooking segments, travel segments, and political insights, was nice, respectably topical, it paid the bills, and it made me locally noticed. But professional respectability, I always believed, came from those sober moments when I delivered the news. This was public service. I anchored the news and it anchored me.

Then, overnight, as these things happen, the station was sold and a shiver ran through the staff. Fox Broadcasting had taken over Metromedia. Rupert Murdoch was making his move from print to broadcast media. Oh, the lectures I got, warning me about him. Harold Evans, the former editor of the London *Times,* came on Panorama and told me—off-camera—about the way Murdoch had handled editorial policy after he'd taken over the London *Times.* Murdoch was a killer, Evans said.

What would I call him? Mister Murdoch? He was, after all, a billionaire a few times over, as well as my boss. I didn't want to grovel, though. He would call me Maury. No doubt about that. He definitely wasn't going to call me Mister Povich.

Had he been knighted? Maybe it was Sir Rupert, or Lord Rupert, or Your Grace. I should have checked the clips. It always pays to do your research. No, this was silly. I'd spoken to presidents and moguls and hot movie actors and I'd called them by their first names. What was the big deal? Besides, the guy's Australian. They call everybody "mate" down there, for heaven's sake.

That settled it. It would be Rupert.

All of this could not have come at a worse time. The age of my wandering was over. I had spent eight years on the road

and left my ego splattered on the streets of four major cities—
Chicago, San Francisco, Los Angeles, and Philadelphia. True,
I had a small cult following who appreciated my television
style, which was a personal version of delivering the news—
raised eyebrows and an attitude of amused and tolerant skepticism. But the great and vast American network audience
wanted something less subversive, something they could regard
as cooperative and objective. It was not in me to report White
House lies as factual. I was a quirky cactus in television's flat,
desert landscape.

Personally, my life had settled down after the usual squall
of domestic turmoil. My first marriage was over long ago and
I had sailed into a state of bliss. It had taken some doing.

By the start of 1984, I was courting Connie again. We had
moved past being a "serious item," but were still vague about
the future. Then came the long vacation, which is rare in our
business. We had a languid stay on the Amalfi coast of Italy.
We stopped in Greece and in Crete and tasted the European
cultural grace, where news is not an urgent thing that jolts you
every half hour with fresh and frightening bulletins about the
world's latest calamity. The news settles gently in Europe,
with a shrug. Somehow it seems less deadly.

I had come home tanned and filled with the wisdom of the
Parthenon. I was not the hot network anchor I had always
yearned to be. I would never be that person. But I had made
peace with myself and it was not so bad. The mental cramps
were gone. I hosted a respectable, eclectic talk show in the
nation's capital, and if I did not have a high Q-rating in Omaha
or Toledo, there were worse fates in life. I anchored the late
news and there was a growing satisfaction in my late and
comfortable success.

It was a sweet season in our lives. Connie was living in New

York and we met on weekends. She had her career and I had mine and the only thing that hovered over my head with some unquiet ache was the question of marriage. It was an unresolved and unspoken issue between us. There were times when she was ready and I wasn't and there were times I was ready and she wasn't. And one day in the autumn of 1984, she called me up and said we could get married now. When I asked how come, she answered, calmly, "Because I found a dress."

Now we were married, she was still living in New York, and I had become resigned to this air-fare marriage. Then came the day, eighteen months later, when my news director, Betty Endicott, came in after the ten o'clock show and said, "Rupert wants to see you. Tomorrow. First thing."

My first thought as usual was, "What did I do wrong?" Then I thought it was a joke, but Betty assured me she wasn't kidding and I said, okay, I'd hit the ten o'clock shuttle. She replied rather pointedly that the shuttles started at seven. "I'd be on the first one; the flunky who made the call and ordered you there didn't sound as if it was something they wanted to discuss. He sounded like a bugle call."

By the time I got to New York and walked into the Fox offices, I was all revved up. I was ushered into a conference room and there were four people there, none of whom I had ever seen before. Except one. Standing off to the side in this kind of makeshift conference room was Rupert Murdoch. He walked over and said, "Maury, happy to see you, glad you could come."

And I said, "It's a pleasure to meet you, Mister Murdoch."

I could see at a glance that he was not what I had expected. He wore a serious and dangerous brow, and spoke softly, politely, minimally, like a Mandarin demigod. Like a Mandarin, however, I knew he could cause men to tremble with a twitch of his finger, lop off heads and uproot populations with a sigh of disappointment. What was I to make of him?

We all sat down and the meeting started. As Rupert spoke, his words were soft and I did not realize until they exploded all around me that they contained professional dynamite.

"We intend to start a new show," he said. "Here, in New York. If it works, we'll put it on the other Fox stations, and then across America. It is going to be unique. You will be the host. So you will not be working in Washington this summer."

I replied: "You don't quite understand. I anchor the news for the most profitable, most successful station in all of Fox."

"That's right," he said. "And you're going to be taking some time off. If it doesn't work, you'll be back there in the fall. Think of it as a summer vacation."

I said it didn't sound like much of a summer vacation to me.

He smiled, but he did not laugh. A wintry smile with no hint of joy. I could see that there was no appeal from decisions already made. And yet I was constrained to push back—something in my nature bristled at the closed nature of the case.

What kind of a show will this be? I asked.

A news show that will make news and break news, he said. Unique.

I was stupid. I said, this is what you brought me here for? It sounds like every other television news show I've ever heard about. What's different?

He looked at me with those cool, deadly eyes and replied simply, "You'll work it out."

And when will you want this program to go on the air?

A man introduced as Ian Rae jumped in. He said in about a month, which was crazy. Starting up a television show took time—a year, six months, at least. Nobody did that kind of thing in a month. You had to get staff, you had to get stories, you had to have trial runs.

Or two weeks, said Murdoch. If you can.

He turned and escorted me around the table. "Peter Brennan has been working in Australian television and he's worked on some of our magazines. Ian Rae was the editor and publisher of the *Star* magazine. J. B. Blunck has been in graphics and was at the *Village Voice*. You will find those stories that work. I have to leave now."

Before he vanished—no doubt to transform another rib of American industry—I said goodbye. I had gathered up my courage and was not going to be cowed.

"We'll see each other again, Maury," he said, heading for the door.

"Nice meeting you . . . Rupert," I called after him.

And he was gone.

I was alone with the brain trust. They were under Rupert's orders, which meant that nothing was to stand in their way. If Rupert said we went in such and such a time, we went. And, suddenly, I sensed a freshness in the air. I was bowled over by the sheer audacity of it all. Nobody mentioned focus groups or consultants or marketing research. These guys were so casual, as if nothing could be easier. They were fearless: Murdoch's daredevil squadron, heading into the unknown without parachutes. I sat there in a daze, listening to the song of these men who were not ground down to mush by conventional wisdom.

I have been on shows where, when something comes up, everything stops until it's settled. Not with these guys. They bypassed problems like enemy strongholds. "We'll fix it later, let's just keep moving." That sort of attitude became contagious, and it didn't take long before I was one of the headlong plungers, thinking that a problem wasn't a rock in the water, but something we'd come back to. I, too, forged ahead.

Something was alive in that room and it was exciting. I could sense the show taking shape in the midst of this happy madness. If we had to, we would put it together with chewing gum and rubber bands, but by God, we are going on the air!

The sound of their voices scared me a little bit, though. It was this Aussie dialect talking about doing American television. Brennan said something like, "Well, we can always rely on Vox pops." And I said, what the hell is that? And they all turned to each other and said, "Oh, what do you call it here? Right, man on the street."

Then he said, "We have to get autocue." And I said, what's autocue? He said, "Oh, what do you call that here? TelePrompTers?"

Right. TelePrompTers. We forged ahead.

I was a little skeptical about the name. There was the possibility of a double entendre because of the use of the word "affair." Everyone waved off the objection. Ian assured me that *A Current Affair* was the name of a very successful show in Australia, a kind of *Nightline* Down Under. Besides—and here was the infallible argument—Rupert loved it. I got the idea.

Rupert had also been very emphatic about developing a singular sound to open the show. Something distinctive. He had been impressed by the ticking clock that opened *60 Minutes.* He said that when you heard that sound, no matter where you were in the house, you were drawn to the television set. He wanted something equally magnetic.

Eventually, J. B. Blunck, the visual genius who had done

so much at the *Village Voice,* would come up with the orange triangle logo. Then he brought out something that was, to say the least, peculiar. With the help of a production house, he took the sound of a golf swing and one of those old-fashioned paper cutters they used in schools, and ran it through a synthesizer. It was jarring, interesting, compelling. We all loved it. It sounded like "Bo-ing! . . . K-chung."

"Let's give it a name," Brennan said.

"We'll call it the Ka-Chung." He smiled. "After Connie."

We talked about when I'd move up from Washington, and they said soon. Start cleaning out your desk right away so we can work together on assembling a staff.

Betty Endicott had heard the news even before I got back to Washington. Everyone had. They had champagne and toasted my future ascent as if they had seen it already. They slapped me on the back and congratulated me and then Betty and I went into her office and closed the door. Betty said that this was a great chance for me. I had a potential—she'd always sensed it. Then she told me something I had already guessed. I had not been the first choice. They had wanted a name, like Geraldo or Tom Snyder, someone outrageous, but those people had demanded huge contracts. And I was already in the family.

"So how much are you getting?" she asked.

"They never mentioned money," I replied.

She looked shocked. Then she nodded. "I don't think you're going to get any extra money. Not if you didn't get that straight up front. Rupert doesn't hand it out easily."

"Yeah, okay, maybe you're right, but I got one thing straight."

"What's that?" she asked.

"I called him Rupert."

Chapter
Four

Duri my initial meeting with the Murdoch brain trust in New York, I had sneaked out once to call Connie and tell her the news. She had just started a show called *1986*, which was going to be split between Washington and New York, and she had been thinking of moving to Washington. Now I was going to move to New York.

"Guess what?" I said when I got her on the phone.

She was always a little apprehensive when I bounced up into her ear with that enthusiasm of mine.

"What?"

"I think you're going to have a house guest this summer," said I. She didn't expect it. Maybe she didn't even want to believe it. Don't get me wrong—we loved each other. We liked being married. We just didn't know if we could live together. It had always been a weekend marriage. She had her ways and I had my ways and there was just a slight bubble of apprehension in her reaction. She was a woman of tidy closets and folded things. I was a flinger of socks. It had worked so far, but maybe it was because of the separate nature of our lives. Now we would be intensely together and that made us both slightly nervous.

When I asked what she thought about the show, she was enthusiastic, and I knew that she meant it because she believed in me. But hers was not an opinion without bias. I had come to know Connie when she had been a kid working in Washington, and that first indelible impression had stuck. In her eyes my time in television would come. As it turned out, it would be later rather than sooner.

Now that I was back in Washington, however, away from the party-line enthusiasm of Murdoch's people, I had an attack of nerves. What was I getting myself into? I was venturing far out on a limb so thin it might not even hold someone who was lighter than air. And so I went to see the one person whose opinion I held high. I went to see my father, Shirley.

My father considered me brash. In that undeclared verdict of his middle child's character, I knew that he considered my life not well thought out. Still, he was the man to whom I turned when I wanted approval or advice because, the truth is, I was of his seed and part of me agreed with his hard assessment of me.

Although I could never duplicate it, I admired his staunch habits and his high principles. I have a child's memory of my father bent over his typewriter after a baseball game, suffering for an ending to his story. We are alone in the stadium—just him and me and the telegrapher, waiting to send that last sentence back to the newspaper. Everyone else has gone home and the stadium is dark and I cannot even see the playing field. I am no more than six, silent as wood, holding my breath, waiting for the words to come, which they finally do, as they always do, thank God. The telegrapher winks at me because only we know the secret of my father's heroic agony.

But then, how could he be anything but brave? He emerged from Jewish pioneers who came to this country from the stormy pale of Lithuania near the turn of the century. Instead of taking that well-traveled path to the urban ghettos of New York, his father and grandfather slung packs on their backs and became Yankee peddlers. They marched up the Eastern spine of America until they hit the coast of Maine, with all that unpolluted salt air and flinty democratic tradition. By the time they reached Bar Harbor, they were already New Englanders, imbued with unbending notions of thrift and stony independence. They opened stores or went to work for the government, but whatever they put their hands to, my father's people—and my mother's people, as well, after leaving Poland and settling in Washington, D.C.—worked long and hard and thrived.

My elder brother, David, and my younger sister, Lynn, were loving and dutiful (and devoted to me), but I was the loose cannon, the free spirit who thought, like Willy Loman, I could get by on a shine and a smile. I can remember dinner conversations which had as the topic Maury's latest screwup. I had flunked a test or skipped an assignment or forgotten a chore. The family would sit around the table speculating, in a very sober and strictly academic and completely loving manner, on why it was that Maury just couldn't seem to get the hang of it.

I tried to soften things, saying hey, maybe I'm not as smart as you think I am, and my father would laugh and say that I was exactly as smart as they thought I was. Once, much later, when I had him on television, I said, Look, Dad, there's this middle-child syndrome, where the middle child is oppressed, and he laughed and said he knew all about the middle-child syndrome: "You exploited it."

And when I flunked out of college, I sat in the back of my father's car as he and my mother drove me home, and felt the full weight of his scowling disapproval.

It was a two-and-a-half-hour drive and it took at least eight days. The only sound I remember is his intermittent comments, declarations that I had lost my sense of values . . . I had no idea of what responsibility was . . . I was throwing my life away. . . .

When we got home, I opened the door, and there my sixteen-year-old sister, Lynn, burst into tears. Until then she'd been some piece of useless furniture in the house, something I had to tolerate but not necessarily relate to. But when I saw her emotion, I knew that she understood and that she was an ally. At that moment all my feelings for her changed. She was no longer a female pest, she was my own sister. And I loved her all the more.

Eventually I would work my way back to the University of Pennsylvania and graduate; I would rise in the world of radio and television—featherweight occupations compared to the blistering work of print journalism. But I believed that his opinion about me was settled on that brutal ride home from college expulsion. Nevertheless, I needed to know what he thought of the switch from *Panorama* to this undefined, formless show, *A Current Affair,* that strained the boundaries of television's dubious respectability. Would it be another screwup?

"Well, Maury, you know that I think you are smart—smarter than you know," he said. "You have to watch out—but I think you can make this work. Rupert Murdoch is a very savvy man."

That was good enough for me!

Back in New York, the single most important priority became the reporters. Where would we find a staff of high-flying wing-walkers? We didn't want youngsters weighted down with telecant. If they came out of the local station farm systems, they were probably already tongue-tied with dogma—tame pussycats who would know all about standards and practices and nothing about telling a good story. We also didn't want young graduates of university media courses. That's where they fry your imagination and blow-dry your brain. We didn't want a smiling parade of blond lookalikes with perfectly capped teeth and a textbook approach to a story.

Brennan agreed. Definitely. We wanted meat-eaters. There is a wonderful expression used by the Australians to describe squeamish reporters who approach a story delicately and never reach the front door. They say such reporters "knock on the grass." We wanted people who would pound down the doors. One thing we knew for certain—we weren't going to raid the staff at Fox News. Except for Dunleavy. But he's an exception to all the rules.

Steve Dunleavy had been Murdoch's man at the *New York Post,* and ran it like a pirate. He'd go out with a cutlass and slice open anybody who got in the way of a story. Blood and gore, sex and scandal, that's what he wanted on the *Post*'s front page. It disturbed a lot of people, but Steve didn't mind disturbing anyone, except Rupert. Some fierce nugget of loyalty toned him down when it came to "the boss." He'd tell anyone else on earth to go to hell, but not the boss.

Before the boss sold the *Post,* he moved Dunleavy to television. Steve didn't know anything about television, but that didn't matter. Steve didn't know he'd be fine on the tube. But the boss knew.

Steve's an Australian from the wrong side of the tracks in Sydney, an outcast's outcast. His father was a photographer from the hard, knock-down school of Australian journalism. There's a story they tell about Steve's father and it doesn't matter if it's true or not. Steve's father, an oppressed, working-class newspaper stiff, was in a crowded elevator in Sydney with the money crunchers—the accountants. According to the story, it was a very, very crowded elevator. The kind where everyone looks up or away to avoid breathing in someone's face. Steve's father was standing next to a man who had made his life miserable, attacking his expenses, challenging his bar tab. So he unzipped his fly and peed on the man's leg. It was too crowded for anyone to move, and when they all spilled out of the elevator, the man was shaking his leg, which was soaked with urine. Everyone else assumed the accountant had done it to himself and fled for cover.

Maybe that's apocryphal, but it tells you something about the man that people believe it. What is true is that Dunleavy's father locked his son in the closet to beat him to a story. But then Steve slashed his father's tires to beat him to another story. That's the kind of family from which he emerged.

Steve spent twenty years in the Far East, bought his suits in Hong Kong, and wore them until they came back into style. He smoked like a fiend and drank like a fish and never dogged it. He didn't knock on the grass. He didn't do anything half-heartedly. He was a tireless, semimodern swashbuckler with a

1950s pompadour and no front tooth. He carried a spare tooth in his pocket for the times when he had to go on camera. He'd pack the false tooth down into his gums with Krazy Glue, then take it out after he had finished taping. He violated every convention and custom of television wisdom—he wasn't handsome, he wasn't clean-cut, he wasn't young, he wasn't well-spoken. He had no sense of the camera or how television worked. But he was passionate and determined and had one irreplaceable and transcending talent: he recognized a good story in a heartbeat. It made up for everything else.

However, the brain trust planned to keep Dunleavy's name out of it at first. For one thing he was Australian and they wanted to give this program an American look. For another, Dunleavy was too closely associated with Murdoch, and Murdoch had that nasty, no-holds-barred tabloid reputation. That's where I came in. I was the spokesman. I would be the host and the front man who would take the questions from the press. I would be the person interviewed about the program. I had certain advantages, because the people who knew me associated me with legitimate, respectable news. *Panorama* had a dignified name in the industry and that was a great advantage for these toothless, street-fighting Aussies.

Over the next few weeks we put together a staff of twenty producers, reporters, and researchers, a team of combustibles, a television dirty dozen, and I was the guy who was supposed to hold it together. The Australians were marked forever by the historical fact that they were the children of criminals, their nation having been founded as Britain's penal colony; they regarded themselves as hereditary outcasts. The Americans—homegrown rebels recruited from small-market exile—were network pariahs because of some inherent streak of unreliability or insubordination. We were bound together by an undi-

minished and happy zest for vulgar truth. No comforting eu-
phemisms, no sappy evasions—life, in all of its messy incarna-
tions was, for us, endlessly fascinating. Somewhere along the
line, each of us had been thwarted by those careful guardians
of taste and style known in the industry as "the suits." Each
of us had run up against the brittle rules of engagement in the
timid news divisions of local stations ("Don't take sides";
"Don't show emotion"; "Be sure to get both sides").

There was an underground of vagabond journalists running
around the country, booted from one market to the next, a pool
of talent that would appeal only to an outlaw network. There
was David Lee Miller, he of the cellular phone, one of those
strange people who enter television almost as an afterthought.
Miller had started out to be a lawyer, but somewhere along the
way he had been bitten by the bug. Professionally, he was
fearless in a terrified sort of way. His fears were common and
ordinary—he was afraid of showing a pimple on camera—but
he was a samurai who walked unarmed into enemy camps. He
did not hesitate to infiltrate the Ku Klux Klan, who kept
looking at his vaguely Semitic features and asking guarded
questions to see if he was really a Jew.

Before he joined the staff, David had been working as a
reporter for a station in Cleveland. He was undercover—but
then we're all undercover when you think about it. It happens
that David has a talent for the role. He's young and handsome,
but in an ordinary, nonthreatening sort of way. So he was
undercover, staked out in front of a chop shop in the middle
of the night in an inclement section of town. His soundman,
Ron, was asleep in the back. The soundman was the only one
authorized under union regulations to drive the van. David was
alert and on duty and it was very quiet until he suddenly felt
the van begin to rock. The people from the chop shop, it

seemed, had caught on to the surveillance and were outside rocking the van and screaming, "Hey, we're going to get you!"

David began to feel the van tilt, as if it were ready to turn over. He sensed danger.

Nonplussed, David leaped into the driver's seat and was relieved to find that Ron had carelessly left the key in the ignition. He thought: No one will complain. This was, after all, an emergency. The chop shop criminals were rocking when he started to roll, but they did not give up. They gave pursuit. They leaped into a Camaro—undoubtedly spliced together from a dozen stolen Camaros—and followed the van along the Cleveland streets, trying to bump it into a steel beam. David took the microphone of the van radio and tried to call for help: "Hello, KQI 361 to desk, this is Unit Seven with an emergency!"

It was early Sunday morning and the streets of Cleveland were empty and the Camaro was bumping the van, trying to drive it off the road, like a real car chase in the movies, only these guys were all certified maniacs. With written proof of their violent offenses.

The desk at the station picked up David's call for help, but this was the football season and the Sunday morning of a Browns home game, and they did not appreciate being bothered by radio calls when they were busy laying down cables for the big game.

"Stay off the air, Unit Seven, we're setting up for a Browns game."

David was trying to drive and to scream at the same time. "No, no, KQI 361, this is Unit Seven with a real, honest-to-God emergency!"

The desk was not impressed. However, some union drivers were in the cafeteria having lunch. These guys were members of the National Association of Broadcast Employees and Technicians—a very strict union—and they had a radio in the cafeteria on which they monitored radio traffic while they ate. Someone heard the transmission from the car-and-van chase and got angry. He picked up the microphone:

"Hey! Who's that driving Unit Seven? Is that Miller? Is that you, David Miller, operating one of our vehicles? Miller, you're not authorized to operate Unit Seven. Where's Ron?"

"I'm being chased by criminals, KQI 361!"

"Miller, this is KQI 361—put Ron on the line."

"He's in the back, about to die!"

Meanwhile, the van had been pretty well bashed and bent, and would probably need a chop shop to put it back together. Police highway units had surrounded the van and emerged, guns drawn. The chop shop cowboys were screaming that Miller was trying to kill them, that they were merely trying to get away and save their own lives, and they were prepared to swear out a complaint.

So the cops arrested Miller and charged him with assaulting the Camaro.

You've got to like that kind of downtrodden character. The charges were eventually dropped, but Miller's contract with the station was not renewed. He was too brave and brash for them. He was our kind of guy.

Another day, I walked into Brennan's office, and sitting there was Rafael Abramovitz, in his ponytail and beard and passionate views. A civil rights lawyer in his late forties, Abramovitz had won a few awards for documentaries and was looking for a job as a producer, but there was something frightening about the man. He held everyone else on earth in contempt, had opinions that he dangled like swords, swaggered in his chair—and yet he was a fresh wind in the face. He was passionate and brilliant and had a knack for finding ways to do stories that everyone else said could not be done. He had a thick European accent, spoke several languages, and could walk on coals, if you believed his own patter. There was no reason to hire him or like him, yet he was an asset and a jewel who could make us all weep.

Not long after he started, Rafael went to Mississippi to do a prison story about a miscarriage of justice. While he was there, it so happened that they were going to execute a condemned prisoner, and Rafael was picked as the pool reporter to witness the execution. He came back and described it for us, in all its infinite cruelty and human degradation—and we were touched. Because we were not fools, we taped his description and it was great television: very moving, very professional. When you watched, you forgot about his accent and his ponytail and his cowboy boots. You paid attention to the eloquent writing and the power of the human heart. For all of his madness, Rafael was a kind of poet. He was our Old Testament prophet who thundered and raged and kept moral imperatives on the agenda. More about Rafael and Gordon Elliott and all the rest of them later.

We were assembling a strange staff, sniffing out our weaknesses, muttering ideas about the show. Meetings were halting and passionate, although strangled by the fact that we did not know what we were going to do. There were a few rules: we were determined to break out of the usual mold and come up with something different. But we didn't have much time and we had no firm grasp of the "concept."

Always, I was thinking about the show. I knew that we were not going to chase fires, we were not going to attend City Hall hearings, and we weren't going to deal with the draining day-to-day news process. But what *were* we going to do? I had no idea. Not yet.

We did get one break. The premiere of the show was pushed back to July 28. That gave us five whole weeks to play with.

During those five weeks I tried to join the brain trust. They were peculiar and had complementary strengths. Rupert called Brennan "the gypsy" for good reason. Brennan went in and out of organizations for Rupert like a nomad. For all his diminished attention span, he had a great tactile sense of where to steer this show. Rae was Murdoch's hound; he would do what he was told. Blunck was the graphics man—young, maybe thirty, maybe a little older, not much meat to his life, but he understood art and operated on the cultural fringe of visuals. His synapses had undergone the shock therapy of the New Age.

We had until the end of July to pull it all together, and we were scrambling for stories. The first show would set the tone—but what was that? In our desperation we got some stuff in the can, a few tired old clichés in case we drew a blank. I actually went to City Hall and interviewed Ed Koch, who was then the Mayor of New York City. It was boring. It wasn't Ed's fault—he didn't know what the show was supposed to be about or he would have been outrageous. God knew he was capable of it. I knew Ed from Washington when he had been a congressman, but that didn't help. We sat in the Blue Room and we talked and he didn't tell me anything new or interesting—he was saving that for a new book, I guess. We didn't want to open the show with a lame excuse for an interview, so we put it on the shelf for some later time when a boring interview wouldn't brand us as nerds.

We still did not have our first blockbuster story. Nobody else seemed concerned. We sat in The Racing Club and swilled beers and Brennan would reach over and put his hand on my arm and smile and say, "Not to worry, mate."

Chapter
Five

Not to worry. A lifetime of journalism and here I was, staring at the abyss, about to fall flat on my face. How did I get here anyway? I groaned, leaning on the bar. What miscreant life had brought me to this pass?

I didn't just drift into this business. I was a homegrown, second-generation journalist.

How could I be anything but a reporter when I grew up in a world enthralled by the glamour of the news business? To this day I can see my father hobbling off a plane in his war correspondent's uniform, an injured hero returning from the battlefront after World War II. At the sight of him we were choked with inexpressible pride—my mother and my brother and kid sister and myself—and swollen by the sheer bravery and zeal that surrounded his job. It was like a perfume that lingered in our house, influenced the dinner table, and left us all besotted with the after-scent of his social nobility. And it was not just the wounds of war. As a committed integrationist, my father pushed for black players on the Washington Redskins football team. He wrote a brave and quietly furious lead when the football great Jim Brown scored five touchdowns against the stubbornly all-white Washington Redskins. "Cleveland's Jim Brown integrated the Washington Redskins' end zone five times yesterday."

Thus, a social conscience was proudly implanted in those early, angry stands that my father took. It seemed to go with the art.

Shirley Povich became a journalist because of golf. After World War I, Bar Harbor, Maine, where the Poviches had traveled and settled and set up a store of their own, became a summer resort for American millionaires, a version of Newport or the South of France. The great families built summer castles in my father's backyard, Rockefellers, Vanderbilts, and Strauses, escaping from the oppressive summer heat to that high, rocky New England coast. And with them came their recreations.

My father worked as a caddy on the local golf course. On an unusually hot day in August of 1919, when Shirley was thirteen years old and no one else wanted the job, he carried the clubs for Ned McLean, who owned the *Washington Post*. Later, Ned would get tangled up in the Teapot Dome scandal, but before his downfall, in that summer after World War I, when the nation was running a high speculative fever and the stock market gushed money, he was at the apex of his fortunes.

Ned McLean was a stubby man of great influence, but his true passion was for golf. He even had his own private golf

70

course built around his home in Washington. On that particular sultry afternoon in August, when everyone else was swimming, with my father at his side, Ned hit a ball in the rough. My father—even then, a sturdy, reliable boy—went after it without hesitation or complaint. He became McLean's caddy for the next three summers. The publisher was so impressed by my father's spunk and grit that he came to my grandmother's house after my father's high school graduation and made her an offer. He would take Shirley to Washington and put him to work on his newspaper, thus assuring his future. It was a time when such things were possible, when odd propositions were not too far from our Horatio Alger expectations, when people were innocent and not every act of kindness was immediately examined for an ulterior motive.

We already had family in Washington working for the government—scholars who took advantage of the impartial civil service tests and were appointed to the secure, midlevel government bureaucracy. My grandmother, not wanting to stand in my father's way, agreed to the offer. In 1922 Shirley went to Washington, where Ned McLean proved to be as good as his word and put him to work. By 1926 my father was the sports editor of the *Washington Post*. That whole episode may have given a false, but nonetheless glittering, hue to our family lore. I grew up thinking of journalism as a thing of infinite possibilities and endless sparkle. In journalism there was always something new, always something to turn to the light and catch a change in the colors. And the truth is that over the years, nothing has altered that rosy view.

I was also bedazzled by Washington. Growing up in the nation's capital, I was under the spell of events. Whatever happened in the world achieved a kind of exaggerated importance, heightened by the illusion that I was in the center of it.

An opinion uttered aloud had an echo, or so we felt, those of us who brushed every day against congressmen and senators in the street.

And the style of the city imposed itself upon my character. Washington was a formal town, a Southern city where people spoke in oblique musical accents and there was a polite undertone to all conversations. Men were called "sir" and women addressed as "ma'am." The fragrance of manners seemed to soften the blunt facts of life, and that was an attractive trait for people who would enter broadcasting. That Southern evasiveness would be counted as charm on the air.

I had certain natural inclinations that propelled me into the business. The fact is, I was likable. It was a blushing but indisputable truth, one which gave my parents no end of grief because I was able to smile my way out of so many jams. It was not a small factor in my career. Being likable gave me access to places from which more sour personalities were barred. It made me welcome.

I started in the business in the summer of my sixteenth year. I was still in high school in 1955 when it dawned on me that I would never be a professional baseball player. I just wasn't big enough or fast enough or talented enough or dedicated enough to pass through the crucible that separated the sandlot champions from the hard professionals. Through my experiences with the Washington Senators, I knew what it took to be a major league ballplayer. I still took infield practice with them and there was no mistaking it. They were gifted with natural athletic grace, and as good as I was and as hard as I worked, I knew that I would never achieve that thoroughbred quality that took your breath away. So I did the next best thing and elbowed my way into journalism, where I could be a paid and appreciated observer.

One thing I knew right away was that I couldn't compete on my father's turf. I would always be compared to someone at the peak of his power. So I began to hang around the broadcasters. In the summer of my sixteenth year I asked a fellow named Bob Wolff if I could work for him. To my amazement he agreed, and he also agreed to pay me. Not much—a few bucks a week, and it came out of his own pocket—but a paycheck just the same. He was one of television's first sportscasters, and he had a pregame show in Washington that was shot on film—dugout chatter, interviews, that sort of thing. In fact, this show was called *Dugout Chatter*.

One of my first jobs was to tell the waiting ballplayers "you're next" to be on the air.

On the second day, my father asked me, "So, sonny boy, what are you doing for Bob Wolff?"

"I'm the assistant producer."

It didn't take me long to seize creative titles in the TV business.

I became Wolff's assistant and gofer. We filmed the shows well in advance of the games and I began to get behind the camera, see how it was done and develop an eye. It was incredible. As soon as I saw the possibilities of television, all the disappointment of not being a player vanished. There was no sadness, only the excitement of a new adventure.

I would watch Bob Wolff, how he conducted himself, how he carried himself and spoke. I carried around a fifty-pound tape recorder and practiced for the time when I too would be on the air. I stopped saying "slidin' " and said "sliding." I rounded out my words and learned the art of painting pictures with words to fill a hole in time.

The decision to become a broadcaster in fact came during my senior year in prep school. I guided the school's baseball team around Tinker Field in Orlando to watch spring training, and as I led them around and they took some infield practice and shagged some flies with a real major league ball club, I did some play-by-play on my recorder. Although it was a gag, I knew that I could do it. It wouldn't be easy; I knew that nothing in my life was going to be easy. There would be no shortcuts to success, I was going to have to take the great Northern route to be satisfied.

This is true in broadcasting, and it is true in every aspect and cranny of my life.

Bob Wolff had played baseball at Duke University, and after serving in the Navy during the war, he had been hired by the DuMont company to do his television show on an experimental basis. He was tall, very youthful-looking, and the older broadcasters in town didn't have much regard for the new kid. He was too young, he hadn't paid his dues, he wasn't a member of the club.

Broadcasting is that kind of business. You are always threatened. There is not a moment in which a new person comes in when everyone else doesn't feel the chill of a new threat. Today's new guy is tomorrow's me. I've watched people come in for interviews and the heads all turn and follow the guy; you can read the thoughts and the fear in the eyes of the old hands. And the most frightened person of all is the anchor. He or she can always feel the ambition and energy crowding him out. It is understandable. Anchoring is a slippery job and you are never on solid ground.

Wolff may have been the new guy, but he had other assets. He did his homework, he worked hard, he made friends with the players, and he taught me things that I have carried with me over the years: a sense of accuracy, of fairness—and of responsibility.

My job was to run around, get material from the dugout chatter and bullpen gossip, and feed it to him on the air. I fed him intricate facts about a guy who hit right-handers better than left-handers, or who slumped in June. I had to tell him who the new pitcher was coming in before the PA announcer told the crowd at the field. When I failed to get the name right, however, or when I couldn't read the number, he felt that I wasn't doing my job and therefore he wasn't doing *his* job. Responsibility.

I spent five years with Bob Wolff, and it wasn't until 1961 that I finally got on the air myself, after the team had moved to Minnesota, and Bob and I had followed. It was a radio game in Detroit. Bob was sharing the mike with Ray Scott. That night Scott was off to do football, and Bob had to catch a plane after the early innings to do a Madison Square Garden event.

There I was alone with the mike, which meant I was more alone than ever before. I got through the seventh and eighth innings. In the ninth, up stepped Harmon Killebrew, the Twins slugger. The play-by-play went like this: "Killebrew digs in at the plate: Here's the pitch. Killebrew swings . . . he hits a big one . . . and it's gone . . . it's over the left stands . . . it's OUT of the stadium. It's the longest home run of my BROADCASTING CAREER!"

Which was literally true.

In 1962 I graduated from the University of Pennsylvania after a somewhat harrowing academic career, and married my fiancée, Phyllis Minkoff. We had been going steady ever since I'd met her on a blind date three years before, and been smitten with her tall, Lauren Bacall looks. For a good deal of the time I had been going with Phyllis—a tolerant, saintly woman—there had been unspoken understandings between us, about which, in my elusive fashion, I had avoided thinking. One night, during my senior year at Penn in 1962, I was playing bridge with the guys when a phone call came in the middle of a hand. My friend Ed Jacobson said, "It's Phyllis." I took the call at the table, while I was looking at my cards, and the way they remember it, I held the receiver in one hand, the cards in the other, and this is how the conversation went: "Yes, Phyllis . . . Yes, Phyllis . . . Yes, Phyllis . . . Yes, Phyllis. Goodbye, Phyllis."

When I hung up, the guys were dying to know what that had been all about.

I said as far as I could remember, Phyllis had said she was sick and tired of going around in this indefinite state and she wanted to clarify our relationship.

"So?" yelled the guys.

"She said we had to get engaged. . . . Whose turn?"

Phyllis and I rented a small apartment in Silver Spring, Maryland, she got a job teaching junior high school in Washington, and eventually I landed a $75-a-week job grinding out press releases as assistant publicity director at WWDC, a 5,000-watt radio station. But I was not on the air. It was a grueling job, and not very elevated, but I was determined to break into legitimate reporting. Sooner or later, I believed, they would discover me. It had to happen. In the winter of 1962 I got a break.

The station never had any sporting events, but that fall they got the Redskins football games, and Bill McPeak, the Redskins coach, was handed a postgame show. He was supposed to offer his assessment of the game from the locker room, and he wasn't so bad, but one day I was asked to hold the micro-phone and pose questions to McPeak. I took it very seriously and mustered all the discipline my father and Bob Wolff had taught me. I went to the game and studied the plays and did my homework. It was little different from what I'd been doing for years with Bob Wolff, but I was producing it. I was into it. I was an interviewer. I was a reporter. It was heaven.

Heaven paid an extra $5 a week.

Soon I got a chance to write five-minute newscasts on the midnight shift, and I was in my glory. I wrote midnight bulle-tins for insomniacs and held a live mike on a postgame football show and it was a constant thrill. While everyone slept, I was a sentry, listening for a shift in the earth's plates.

It wasn't long before I got a raise to $100 a week because I worked hard. I worked Saturdays, Sundays, Easter. And I learned the art of living on the air. There were rules and codes and they were not all written down. One announcer went on the air at Easter, annoyed because he had to work on a holiday, and when he delivered the newscast he said: "This is Easter Sunday, 1963, the day of the alleged resurrection of Christ."

Alleged!

He was a practicing Christian and he did it as a prank because he thought no one was listening in the middle of the night and he'd get away with it. But the phones roared with indignation. People were very touchy about what was said about God, especially on the radio. The fact that it was on radio or television seemed to imbue speech with greater weight, apart from the fact that there was inevitably a larger audience. Many listeners regarded radio talk itself as something almost sacred. That announcer was fired and, for a while, disgraced, and I saw very clearly that there were lines that could not be crossed. Even if you were on FM radio in the middle of nowhere, someone was out there listening and you'd better not utter blasphemy.

Some of the news readers would get very nervous about my quiet antics—putting a funny spin on a congressional story, finding the lighter side of human relations—and they said, "Hey! What are you trying to do?" And I would explain, look, I'm just trying something different.

The news directors themselves were amused. They were Texas liberals—you had them in Washington in the early sixties, helping to change the course of the South. They tended to be lenient and a little wild, and they let me write radical editorials about attempts to redistrict the Maryland Legislature, and they didn't give a damn if I was inflammatory. I'd raise hell about Congress cutting off welfare and school funds for the District of Columbia because Congress controlled the D.C. budget and those Southern rednecks tended to be a little tight with a buck when it came to spending money on blacks. I'd write flaming attacks, accusing Congress of racism and saying that it was another instance of white domination and that it was unconstitutional. And we got action.

Budgets were increased. Gerrymandering was curtailed. And I got a nightly fifteen-minute sportscast. I was bad, but I got better and it wasn't long before the station manager noticed this kid bursting with energy, and I was promoted to a staff job. This was it! I was covering the Hill and the Senate and tracking presidents and I was intoxicated with the notion of being a reporter. It does that to some people. You ride in presidential motorcades, and you get addicted to the tang that comes with being up close to raw power and quick events.

Phyllis stopped teaching after the baby came. Susan had

been born on June 27, 1963. We were living in a two-bedroom apartment in Maryland, but my mind wasn't on it. I raced around town, dizzy with my career. I was doing the news. I won an Associated Press award for a radio documentary on police acts of courage called "Behind the Badge," and on the surface things looked fine. Looking back, I can see that I was troubled and that we had different expectations about the marriage. Not that Phyllis objected to the hours or the obsessive nature of the job. But bad habits took root in those early days and they would eventually cause problems that could not be healed. I developed the habit of neglect. A certain assumption that my job was all-important and that taking care of Maury was a thing of great value. I can see how little waves of resentment were left carelessly behind me in the wake of my great hopes for myself.

The first time I went on the air as a genuine, full-fledged news reporter was in the summer of 1963. Jack Kennedy was going to open up a new highway—I-95—between Baltimore and Wilmington, and I drove up there to cover it by myself. I had a long drive and it was midsummer and hot and I was all excited. I was supposed to call in afterward from a pay phone and file a piece with the Kennedy speech. I was feeling cocky because I knew just which portions of his speech I was going to use and I looked down and my heart fell. I had forgotten to press the record button on the tape recorder.

I felt an overwhelming sense of panic and defeat, but then Pye Chamberlain from UPI audio gave me his tape. It wasn't all humanitarian and selfless. He knew that there might come a time when he would forget to push the record button and I would give him my tape. It is all so competitive, but then there comes a moment when you realize that you are in this lifeboat together.

Within a month came the march on Washington, August 28, 1963. I was the newest reporter and therefore drew the least-important assignment. In the midst of this huge moment in history, I was to cover George Lincoln Rockwell and his twelve neo-Nazi counterdemonstrators. They were pushed to the fringes of the crowd, surrounded by hordes of cops, and nobody cared about them. I, too, ignored Rockwell and his silly counterdemonstration and became one more member of the audience, caught up in the "I-have-a-dream" speech.

On November 22, 1963, I was covering the District Building, the local city hall in Washington. It was two-thirty in the afternoon and I was just coming back from lunch when I saw everyone running around: not with any purpose—just running, almost in circles. The faces were pale and the people were frightened. I stopped one of the guards and asked what happened.

"Kennedy's been shot."

I was scared. The blood must have drained from my face. I knew that if I hesitated, if I allowed myself to dwell on what had happened, I would be lost. I counted to three, took some deep breaths, and called the office. They told me to go to the Hill. Teddy Kennedy was in the Senate there, and when he found out, he said nothing. He was told and then he was gone. I spent the day working the Hill, talking to congressmen, getting interviews. That night I went to the churches and the services all over town. The grief was overwhelming and it was everywhere.

At Andrews Air Force Base, Jackie came off the plane with the casket and her dress all smeared with Jack's blood and that brave, defiant, fierce look on her face, and I bit my tongue to keep from crying. It seemed important to remain stoic. That night I went to the station, and even the people on the job had the grim expression of deep sorrow. It was after midnight and I had been working for sixteen straight hours and everybody was debriefing everybody else on the air. There were cracked voices, a few choked pauses, but it was still pretty professional. The anchors were questioning the reporters and the reporters were questioning the producers, and as I told about Jackie coming off the plane, I started to weep. I was very surprised at myself.

That ended 1963—my introduction to hard news.

Poor Lyndon Johnson became the dreary second husband, trying every which way to please, but hopelessly clumsy. He couldn't hold a candle to Jack Kennedy's eternal flame. And so he fled into Vietnam. Instead of the arms of another woman, he sought comfort in the Asian mud. He got the Kennedy legislation passed, launched the Great Society, and marched far out front with civil rights legislation, and still it wasn't good enough. He was cursed by contrast.

I covered it all. Because of the way things worked, the President of the United States was a local story. He had to sign off on all the local legislation, he ran the town, so I covered the President. One hour I was off covering a robbery and the next I'd be at a White House briefing. I found myself standing next to John Chancellor and Helen Thomas and Roger Mudd—my colleagues.

In June of 1964 the White House announced that an American destroyer had been attacked by North Vietnamese gunboats. I was at the White House that night and I asked what kind of boats they were. I pressed and pressed and the White House spokesman fudged. Everyone in the media pressed the point. What kind of boats would go after an American destroyer? After a lot of backtracking and corrections, these boats that started out very big came down in size until they were just piddling little PT boats, if that, and we knew—we all knew in our guts—that they were lying.

He got away with it, of course, because this was Washington and those committee chairmen were all Southern patriots. Out of that came the Gulf of Tonkin Resolution, and we were lost in Vietnam.

For three years I stayed on that local beat, learning to be a reporter—covering cops, covering the White House, covering everything; learning how to pick out the essential ingredients of a story, finding the cops who were there first, the witnesses who saw it happen, finding the eyes of the neighborhood, the techniques of tracking down a source, making endless calls, running down telephone books. Using common sense on a story. Not genius. Common sense. What's likely. What's unlikely.

If you put the arresting officer's name in the story, you got a friend. If some news editor asked for more information, you went back to the scene—counted the leaves on the trees.

I know that my name helped. Wherever I went—covering local politics or local crime—the *Washington Post* reporters would fill me in. It was a big advantage. Radio guys couldn't spend all day on a story. We were there for an hour and then we had to move on. We had to produce four or five stories in a day. The newspaper reporters immersed themselves in the details. They got to know the story and the people the way you get to know things when you just hang around and grow bored. People tend to grow accustomed to newspaper reporters in those long silences. There are no long silences on radio. Couldn't afford them. No patience. Radio ate patience. I would come onto a scene and get the deepest background briefing possible from the sympathetic print guys on the story. They resented the other radio reporters because they knew that they were making more money and had no attention span and didn't have to dig in like infantrymen to get the story. They didn't have to earn a story. But I was Maury Povich, Shirley's kid, and I had to be okay.

I had fills from the best. I was given deep understanding of the workings of government and the weaknesses of man. I was taught the complexities of human behavior and the subtleties of style. I didn't just glide over an event and see what there was to see and phone it in; I had the whole novel read to me. I was the beneficiary of a literary view of the common world.

At one point the station gave me what was called an Amphi-car. It was an experiment they had leased: a news car that could go into water. I used it to cover the hydroplane races, another time on a drowning. There was a two-way radio in the car and I could broadcast directly from the scene. Very state-of-the-art. Very James Bond. Very silly.

People made fun of it as I drove around town in this strange car with two propellers sticking out of the back, but I was in a business that invited a little ridicule and I didn't care.

I wanted to do hard news. In 1966, when the independent Metromedia television station started a ten o'clock news program I applied, and was hired to do both the news and the sports.

We had a couple of weeks' rehearsal and I thought I had it all straight, and that first night I was terrible. I went into my closing kicker, which was a funny story, and said, "You should have seen it, it was the funniest thing at the Redskins' game," and the floor director ran her hand across her throat, which I took as a literal cut sign that I was out of time. So I said, "But we don't have time for that story today." And I threw it back to the news guys. After the sportscast they tried to cheer me up, told me that it wasn't so bad, but I knew better. The cut sign had not been literal, the floor director had just wanted to push me a little faster.

I was not comfortable on the tube for the rest of that year, but the general manager, Bob Bennett, was ambitious and wanted to make a mark. In January of 1967 he decided that he was going to do something unheard of: he was going to launch a three-hour talk show in the middle of the day, from noon until three. Bennett intended to have two cohosts for this show, a man and a woman. The lead was an announcer he knew from California named John Willis, the woman was a movie reviewer from Boston named Pat Collins, who was making a name for herself by the sting of her remarks. She had even been banned from attending previews at some Boston theaters.

But then he decided that he also needed someone who knew Washington. So he turned to me and said, "You're on."

Panorama was a hodgepodge of physical fitness, travel tips, cooking segments, and politics. Always politics. It was Washington and you could not escape from politics. Phyllis was buying my wardrobe and I was chasing fire engines.

The show was received with cool respect. We were not a huge hit in the ratings, but there was merit and good intentions in the conception, and I loved my role. Willis was in his forties and he was respectful. Pat was cultural. I was the voice of dissent about Vietnam, the young rebel, challenging authority.

Panorama became a fortress of social concerns, controversy, and just plain gossip in the middle of all of the breathless bulletins. The planet was spinning with assassinations, riots, demonstrations, social upheaval. We put Evans and Novak on the air, as well as Pat Buchanan, John McLaughlin, Tom

Braden and Lady Bird Johnson. People who would later make great marks in the industry cut their teeth on our show. Abbie Hoffman and his American flag shirt flew on our show. Nothing was too touchy to touch.

On January 5, 1967, my second daughter, Amy, was born, and we moved to a house in Maryland, but my attention was still diverted.

And during the Watergate hearings, the Senate Committee counsel, Sam Dash, would come on during the noon recess and explain himself on our show. There was that high, flushed excitement of being in the midst of a great moment in history, and a funny thing began to happen: I grew comfortable in front of the camera. Eugene McCarthy called me by my first name. I played with Bobby Kennedy's kids at Hickory Hill. There were bomb threats and backlash, but that was to be expected.

At the time, there was a spunky young secretary working at the station who wanted to be a reporter. When she pushed for a writer's job, her boss agreed, but said he'd have to find her replacement first. So this tough-minded secretary, who was not going to wait around for someone to show up to take over her job, went across the street to the bank. She asked a teller she knew if she wanted to work in television, and when the teller agreed, Connie Chung brought her own replacement in so that she could start writing. This was a young woman intent on making TV news more than just a boys' world.

After the Yom Kippur War in 1973, the Israelis took a beating in the War of Attrition. Terrorism had broken out in the Middle East. In 1974 I was invited to cover it. The Syrians were shelling Israeli villages, and the Israelis were bombing Syrian positions. I phoned an old fraternity brother, Kenny

Elias, who was a cattle farmer in Galilee, and I could hear the bombs in the background. When I went, I found my old friend in battle gear and the mood of the country very bad. There was no enemy to confront.

Through some congressional contacts who thought that I was pro-Israel, I made my way into Lebanon to cover the Arab side. Beirut was a revelation, a beautiful city of cosmopolitan grace, influenced by the French, enriched by oil money, a nest of spies, teeming with merchants and bankers and beautiful women. I spent some time with the Palestinians in the south, where they lived in camps and wore military uniforms and staged border raids against Israel. I realized when I met them that Lebanon was lost. The Palestinians would either take over the country or ruin it. They were not going to stay in the camps. I ate at their table, witnessed their training, and shook under the attack of four Israeli Phantom jets.

I filmed the reports, and afterward—after Nixon left office and after the war coverage—I experienced a kind of emotional crash. There were no more worlds to conquer on *Panorama,* and I began a ten-year quest to rediscover the charge that I had felt when I had first gone into the news business. I had to stumble from city to city and job to job, losing my family in the process, before I would find it again in *A Current Affair.*

Chapter Six

THAT was all. I didn't want to think about those years right now. Maybe later. Right now I had to figure out what in God's name I was going to put on the air for our first show.

I should have trusted Brennan. Somehow he knew we would find a nugget. Even though he hadn't produced his first show on American television, he knew if we started digging around, we would not only find it . . . but it would be in our own backyard, New York.

Among the stories tickling the producers' interest was a juicy rumor of trouble in Chinatown, nothing that had hardened into anything substantial, just something elusive and tantalizing, wafting in the air of the city. Most of us ignorant Occidentals had been led to believe that the members of the Chinese-American community were uniformly family-oriented, highly disciplined, and blessed with inner peace. They did not engage in disruptive antisocial behavior and they definitely did not seek fame and major publicity blowouts. They were model citizens, pointed to by civic scolds as an example of an oppressed people who didn't cause the rest of us a lot of headaches by complaining about their mistreatment.

The truth, as usual, was slightly more complicated. The cop reporters at headquarters, located strategically on the lip of Chinatown in Lower Manhattan, said that a vicious tong war was already underway. Now that the leaders of the Italian Mafia were preoccupied fighting off federal, state, and municipal strike forces, the Chinese tongs were making territorial moves on each other. They wanted to take over the highly lucrative, not to mention financially liquid, drug trade.

To carry out the actual fighting, they were using teenagers, immigrants fresh from Taiwan and Hong Kong, who had no compunction about rough combat. These Hong Kong soldiers had one slight drawback: they were nuts. They'd storm into crowded restaurants and spray everyone in sight with MAC-10s on full automatic. This was extremely bad for the tourist trade, especially for the tourists who got caught in the crossfire.

The nightly news began to run a lot of stories about mysterious gun battles and "reported" gun activity, and "in-depth" profiles about the changing nature of Chinatown, but the truth was that we had no idea who was doing what to whom. We were blind. The tong warlords were not familiar, or even genially idiosyncratic, like the crazy Gallo brothers who had had the charming quirk of keeping a lion in their Brooklyn basement to impress visitors. They weren't dashing like John Gotti, "The Dapper Don," who wore $3,000 suits and threw an annual Fourth of July block party for his neighbors in Queens. Gotti had become a kind of homegrown duke for the cut-rate price of some free hot dogs and hamburgers. His public loved the idea that the cops couldn't stop his illegal fireworks display.

The Chinese gang lords, on the other hand, were very private. However, we had a secret wedge. Steve Dunleavy said maybe we could do a story about the biggest one, the "leader." Maybe he would even give us an interview, although that was unlikely. In any case we could put a face on the story. All we had to do was to find "Uncle Jimmy."

Who in the world was Uncle Jimmy? We all wanted to know.

He looked at us with pity. Here he was, an outsider, and he knew more than us in the room about the mechanics and mobsters of our own society. He knew that Jimmy Chin was the Godfather of Chinatown. Jimmy Chin had the muscle, ran the gangs, and enforced his own brand of law and order: our very own Mao. Of course Dunleavy had learned this from his cop friends.

There is a strange and powerful relationship between reporters and cops. It's not always friendly, but it's always intense. The value of such close contact is beyond measure. When you hang around the squad rooms of station houses, if you're not a fool or a weasel you pick up stories like a tan at the beach.

Once, when I was a young radio reporter in Washington, I'd been sent to the cop shop to hang out. Al Lewis, the wizened old veteran from the *Washington Post* who had been assigned to headquarters before recorded time, was one of those half-breeds—more cop than reporter. Sometimes such people even get called "inspector," an honorific that was useful in obtaining stories, and on that particular morning Al had a beaut. It was too late for him to use in the morning edition of his own newspaper, and he didn't want the afternoon paper to get it and beat him, so he gave it to me because I was a nice boy with an appreciative attitude toward my job. Besides, I was Shirley's kid. The story was about a segregationist mayor who'd come to a convention in Washington and been stung by a black flimflam man. The Alabama mayor had been robbed and left naked, and the cops thought that it was a hoot. They couldn't stop talking about it, because cops are notorious story-tellers and gossipmongers, and the *Washington Post* cop guy picked it up and gave it to me.

Cops and reporters kept careful books and knew how to repay old debts, and nobody had better access to the cops than Dunleavy. They trusted him like a midnight partner. Maybe they sensed something broken about him, and because they deal so intimately with broken men, they gave him things they didn't even share with other police departments. And he gave them back his everlasting word. By the same token, Dunleavy was a sentimental favorite and drank with the cops and listened to their endless woes, and because of that part of his natural inclination, we got an opening story for the show.

Dunleavy had a fair idea of how to cover the Chinatown story. The thing was that Dunleavy couldn't go after Uncle Jimmy himself. It would expose our main source and open us up to that charge of being (God forbid!) Australian. So we sent David Lee Miller out to get the interview with Jimmy Chin. You understand that up until then nobody had ever laid a camera on Uncle Jimmy. Hardly anyone outside of the police intelligence units even knew of his existence. Getting an inter-view would be a major scoop, which was certainly the proper way to launch a new show.

Dunleavy—the most unselfish reporter on earth—handed

his material over to David Lee Miller. He told him where to find Jimmy Chin, how to approach the story, what the salient facts were, the nature of the tongs and how they operated, and how Jimmy Chin controlled the illegal life of Chinatown. Dunleavy gave it away without any thought of credit or payback. He was a true member of a team. His philosophy was: If the show succeeds, we all succeed.

Maybe Brennan and Dunleavy knew we would come through okay and get the story and actually have a show, but I was a wreck. Brennan would say, in his infuriatingly calm way, "We'll have the story, mate!" That was his operating method. If worse came to worst we would go with it even if we didn't get an interview with the man himself. As time began to close in, the deadline for the show approached, and the chances for an interview diminished. I began to worry, in spite of all that Australian calm and bottled beer. Not that David Lee Miller wasn't giving it the college try. He spent day and night prowling Chinatown, talking to sources, making a pest out of himself, and poking his American face into the known secret haunts of people who did not particularly want strange faces hanging around.

David knew, however, that the story of Uncle Jimmy, who was running the Chinatown Mafia, was going to save our first show. He was a man with a mission. He was always a man with a mission.

Two days before the show, we had a lot of background, a lot of information, and a lot of atmosphere. We had interviews with experts from the Police Department who told us in their strangled, official manner about the nature of Chinatown, the increasing levels of violence, and the dangers of the gang wars.

We had the body count and the explanations for the escalating violence. We had plenty about Jimmy Chin's turf. But we did not have Jimmy Chin. Filled with frustration, David finally decided that he was going into the lion's den alone and beard the old bandit. He knew where to find Jimmy's social club, which was in the basement of one of these turn-of-the-century tenements off East Broadway. The Chinese mobs were like the Italian mobs. They spent their days in basement or storefront social clubs, plotting, but sipping tea instead of anisette.

Uncle Jimmy wasn't home when Miller barged into the social club, but David found his Number Two man playing with an abacus and demanded an interview with the boss. Maybe he thought he could bluff his way past the first line of defenses—I can't even imagine the courage it took to perform such an act—or maybe David was moved by that other thing, fear. Not fear of getting killed—fear of failure. He was, as I have said, a man with a mission.

These men were murderers, and it was not inconceivable that for such effrontery they would feed David Lee Miller, little by little, to the fish, but as it happened, the Number Two guy did not kill David Lee Miller. He merely told him, in a quiet but firm voice, to leave. And David left, dropping off his business card like some salesman making calls.

"Will you ask Mister Chin if he will consent to an interview?" called David as he was ushered out of the door.

The Number Two man did not answer.

Frustrated but undaunted, David roamed the streets of Chinatown, unwilling to give up on his assignment—which, to him, was a holy thing. He walked the streets with the camera crew, past the stores with the fresh fish in the windows and exotic vegetables in the bins. The sidewalks were slippery with Shanghai lettuce, and the air rang with the rising conversations, fighting to be heard above the tourist chatter and the rumble of delivery trucks and the general noise congestion. Suddenly, as he walked down Mott Street, David saw, coming at him, surrounded by a cluster of bodyguards, underlings, and seekers, Uncle Jimmy himself.

"Uncle Jimmy! Uncle Jimmy!" David cried, and the old man blinked, looked up and past David Lee Miller, and saw the camera. Instinctively, he got excited and angry and he spat at the cameraman. But he didn't attack David. Somehow, he did not connect David Lee Miller to the technology.

In some strange way David sensed an opportunity.

"Uncle Jimmy! Uncle Jimmy! Could you spare me a moment?"

The way things work in Chinatown is that business is very insular and works in odd ways. Uncle Jimmy was a great man on Mott Street—people leaped off the sidewalk to avoid inconveniencing him. He had the aura of power and the wisdom of ripe years. But he was not of the television age. He did not understand the wild impulse that makes some reporters walk up to dangerous warlords and ask for an interview. It was such a bizarre request that Jimmy Chin looked a little puzzled by such a remarkable question. But then, even more bizarrely, he agreed. The underlings and advisers, bodyguards and seekers, were utterly baffled, but did not dare contradict Uncle Jimmy who, perhaps operating on a higher level of wisdom, was planning to use the instrument of television to advance his interests in the wider world of Western media. Or maybe he was simply befuddled. In any case he told David to come back the next day to the social club that was his headquarters and he would do this thing that was being asked of him, this interview.

At the time I viewed it as nothing short of a miracle.

Brennan had been promoting the story, taking out newspa-

per and television ads and advertising it without any guarante
that it would come true. He had the courage of a true believe
and the nerve of a safecracker. "Never mind, mate, we'll hav
something to put on the air."

Meanwhile, David Lee Miller went back the next day
and—wonder of wonders!—had his interview with Uncle
Jimmy. Granted, it may have not been groundbreaking jour
nalism in terms of candor and revelations—the fact is, the ol
man didn't say anything of any enduring interest; he didn'
even say anything noteworthy—still, David Lee Miller had
accomplished this amazing feat. He had bagged a legendary
and enigmatic figure who had talked to no other television
journalist. He had put the man's image on film, along with hi
voice. In television, what you show is not necessarily as impor
tant as getting an interview with a difficult source. Even if th
source says nothing at all, you can say you got an interview
It has something to do with the nature of television, the me
dium is the message and so forth. And we had Uncle Jimmy
It gave us legitimate bragging rights for sheer enterprise. Dur
ing the interview, Uncle Jimmy tried to come across as a gentle
senior citizen who was not involved in crime, was an innocen
victim of prosecutorial overzealousness, and had been unfairly
depicted in a negative light: the usual strategy of denial tha
will convince thirty-two percent of the audience and confus
sixty-seven percent of the others. It didn't matter. What mat
tered was that David Lee Miller had gotten his interview.

And so we went on the air with our first show and I wa
terrible. Not just a little off, or a bit shaky, or a trifle uncer
tain—a wholesale, full-scale, post-primetime disaster. I had
squeaky voice, sweaty palms, and I was all itches, twitches, an

tics. It is the way I always appear on the first show. I could string together a tape of my first shows and they would blow a hole in the ozone layer. Later, on the second, third, or fourth shows (if there are second, third and fourth shows), I invariably improve. My voice returns to its usual home base—the raspy handiwork of too many cigarettes and too much whiskey—my palms dry up and my skin calms down and my eyes return to focus. I can even do a creditable job of seeming at ease. But opening night is always a disaster.

Nevertheless we all thought that the first show of *A Current Affair* was a great triumph, all in all. David Lee Miller had saved our bacon with the story of Uncle Jimmy. There was a party afterward. Connie was there, a tonic for everyone, especially me. Rupert came by with his brooding well-wishes and that tricky smile of his, congratulating everyone, shaking everyone's hand. Then he took the "family"—Brennan and Rae—into the conference room and locked the door. We all assumed that it would be a helpful critique—possibly pointing out a flaw here, a blemish there, a suggestion or two about graphics—followed by lavish bonuses and universal praise and genuine backslapping. But we were wrong. Rupert was furious. In fact, he wanted David Lee Miller fired on the spot.

It was unbelievable! I was openly stunned when Brennan took me into his office and repeated Rupert's complaint. Rupert was not angry about me, which would have been understandable, something I could support. No, Rupert thought that I was fine. He was convinced that the David Lee Miller segment was a disaster.

Why did he want Miller's head? Because, as Brennan would later patiently explain as I listened agape, David Lee Miller had failed to deliver Jimmy Chin.

Wait a minute, I said, this kid did deliver Jimmy Chin. He

had gotten an interview with him. He had been the only electronic journalist to nail the old guy on tape, to sit him down and get him to answer a few questions. Granted, the answers had been disingenuous, but what the hell would anyone expect? Did Rupert think John Gotti would come on the air and say, "Yes, I am the *capo di tutti capi* of the Gambino family and I order men executed and I live off the earnings of my criminal empire"? No, on the record, Gotti was always a poor sheetmetal salesman who happened to have million-dollar mob lawyers at his beck and call.

Rupert, said Brennan patiently, had lectured his "family" about the nature of his new show. He had not thrown all of this money at us to bring in an "ordinary" program with the usual stories about good guys and bad guys. He wanted a brand-new kind of journalism. Activist. When he said that he expected David Lee Miller to bring in Jimmy Chin, he meant it literally. He expected our reporter to go out and arrest Jimmy Chin. A reporter he had in mind—his kind of reporter—would have clapped kindly old Uncle Jimmy in irons, in full view of his henchmen—which would have made an interesting part of the show if the henchmen didn't gun down Miller and the cameraman and the soundman first—then march him to the Elizabeth Street police precinct, where he would present this known felon, this unrepentant villain, to the desk officer. Swear out a complaint. Press charges. A trophy from an aroused citizenry who were no longer going to tolerate criminals in their midst.

It was an interesting twist on activist journalism. The power to arrest!

Brennan said that it took him and Rae some time to convince Murdoch that it simply wasn't possible, not in America at any rate, not with the current state of civil rights laws and the activity of the American Civil Liberties Union. Not even the intrepid Dunleavy could carry off such a feat. Rupert sat in that room and demanded explanations of why it couldn't be done, exactly. He listened, mumbled, listened some more, shook his head, and pressed his lips. For all its Wild West imagery and vigilante notions, America was not like Australia.

Murdoch had emerged from the session with a scowl. He remained unconvinced. There was a particular show in mind and he saw it in that far-seeing eye of his. His reporter rounded up the bad guys.

We considered it a victory that he was talked out of firing David Lee Miller.

Chapter
Seven

WE existed. *A Current Affair* was a terrifying fact of evening macho journalism in the New York market. The only problem was, whatever secret vision Rupert Murdoch possessed at this point, no one, not even the perennially cheerful and eternally unflappable Peter Brennan, had any reasonable idea of what *A Current Affair* was supposed to be doing in America's living rooms. After poking our heads out of the tube, we remained in some ambiguous stage of fetal television life. As far as I was concerned we were still only a matter of faith.

I needed a more concrete sign. I spoke to my father, mother, brother, and sister and they all had opinions. My father was a much more cautiously cerebral human being than I was, although there had to be a Wild West gambler somewhere in his heart; how else could he be a newspaper cowboy? He had counted on Murdoch's smarts to overcome the risk of my leaving the secure world of *Panorama,* where I shone. His idea, born in the nineteenth-century factory mentality, was always that you didn't give up a good job—you stayed with the company. But once having plunged into *A Current Affair,* he tried to make supportive suggestions, although he still didn't "get it," frankly, and wanted me to be careful. I told him that if you wanted to be careful, you stayed out of television.

He thought that the show should be well researched, well crafted, spotless. I could not explain to him—nor even to my sister, Lynn, a senior editor at *Newsweek*—that that "finished" look was exactly what we were trying to avoid. We didn't want to be Sinatra after the midnight show, with his tie undone as if he were playing to the true fans but was in reality faking spontaneity. I wanted to be Lenny Bruce as anchorman: stream-of-consciousness stories hitting some deep, shocking nerve of truth and recognition.

My family and friends gave their advice, and I listened, and the truth was that I was influenced. I was, in fact, embarrassed by the gaudy nature of some of the stories we were programming for *A Current Affair.* I didn't think that our rundown should be all focused on torrid sex, ruthless murder, and boundless greed. What about social responsibility?

One night, after a long story meeting during which a particularly lurid tale had been received enthusiastically, I closed the office door and said to Brennan, "Look, that story is ridiculous. What about toxic waste and corruption? How can we do silly stories about mad dogs and jealous lovers every night, Peter?"

He looked at me with those bright, squinty little eyes and thought about it. "Well, love, why don't you just say something?"

"But I am. Right now. I'm saying something. Don't you hear me? This is called complaining."

"No. I mean, say it on the air. You got something on your chest, say it. You don't agree with a particular story, disagree. Make a comment. Cut it up. Let the audience know that you're not just a puppet sitting up there. You're on their side. At least the ones who disagree. It'll work, mate, trust me."

It was in fact a brilliant idea. It took them off the hook, because now they could show anything at all, from high-priced hookers to lowdown scams, and they had an automatic disclaimer—me. They covered both sides: the ones who wanted all the gore and glitz and the ones who wanted to express the higher sensibilities—but still wanted to watch.

I knew that television worked by magic. Operating under the surface picture and text was a subtext of deeper, unscripted meaning. Over the years I had learned to express my personal opinion about stories by tossing the audience a set of signals: a lift of my eyebrow, a wag of my head, the raising and lowering of my voice—a flash of what seemed to me like the underlying truth.

Now I could deliver on-air reviews. Nobody could take all that stuff straight. I could lift the curse off UFO encounters with my eyebrow. I could issue wry disclaimers for the stories about the effects of nude beaches and the cavorting at a *Soldier of Fortune* Magazine convention. On the other hand, by the simple act of sounding and looking grave and sober, I could bestow a seal of approval on the substantial stories about grieving parents and sore social issues that deserved respectful attention.

Maybe we were groping forward, but we were moving ahead in first class. We still had the boss's checkbook and the boss's mandate. Rupert did not necessarily agree with what he saw—there was always the threat of that raised eyebrow, which loomed like an open ICBM silo over our future—but he had given his word that we would have a chance to fail. And we were determined to go right ahead and do whatever it was that we were supposed to do. We were all curious to see just what the hell we were going to turn out to be.

Brennan saw to it that we conducted business in style. I remember coming up from Washington, looking over the studio and seeing the equipment, and being impressed by all the great effort and energy that had gone into this makeshift thing. There was Brennan issuing command orders for bigger and better typewriters, high-tech editing machines, intercontinental ballistic coffeemakers, executive-type desks and user-friendly chairs, and whatever the hell else we needed to ensure the triumph of democracy. Everything in an instant, top of the line.

Then I saw the TelePrompTers and gasped.

Something wrong, mate? asked Brennan.

I nodded at the TelePrompTers. They were ancient models, slow, clunky, obsolete relics from the dawn of television. It was like finding a quill in a newspaper city room. I could not say enough about them, and there was Brennan, nodding his head, taking it all in.

Brennan didn't know that much about television—he was basically a print guy—but he knew how to find out. He had friends in every walk of life. If you wanted someone who knew about the law, he knew someone who had a Supreme Court Justice in his pocket. You wanted politics, he had senators, congressmen, mayors . . . whatever was necessary. There's a Brennan fan club out there and everyone who's ever met the guy belongs. So he had J. B. Blunck call up his television supply friends, and J. B. asked them, what's the latest in TelePrompTers and how do I get hold of some?

The next morning, when I came in, the studio contained state-of-the-art TelePrompTers. Not in a month. Not in a

week. The next morning. In big, supernova network operations, it takes a few months to order one of those beauties, and
even then you have to fight like crazy to move the shipment
along. Brennan had five of them the next morning. It was the
way he worked. The man could always get to the heart of the
matter.

So we rolled tape with high hopes, great logistics, superior
TelePrompTers, and waited for it to happen—the story that
would define us, that would tell us and the world exactly what
our show was meant to be. Until that story broke, until we got
onto it and covered it like a blanket, I really didn't get it either.
I thought that we were some bastard version of the six o'clock
news, gussied up with smoke and a synthesizer. As to substance, which was what I yearned for, I still did not have a clue.
Mary Beth Whitehead told me.

It started out as a low rumble in the belly of the news.
Sometimes the great stories break that way, a distant thunder
that registers dimly on our journalistic search-radar. The size
of the case was not instantly apparent in the summer of 1986.
It was just a custody suit. The adoptive parents of an infant
girl were trying to regain custody of their child from the birth
mother. But there were complications. For a sum of money,
Mary Beth Whitehead had signed a contract to be the surrogate mother for William Stern's child. She had been artificially
inseminated with his sperm. Now she wanted her child. So did
William Stern. Technically they were both parents.

There was nothing spectacular in the opening salvo of facts:
a mother had changed her mind. As it began to work its way
through the New Jersey courts, however, we all began to see
the great dramatic freight that this story carried. It was nothing

less than an emotional blockbuster. The plain ingredients were class and the natural order of things.

According to the facts conceded by both parties, William and Elizabeth Stern, a childless couple belonging to the upwardly driven professional class, had elected to seek a surrogate mother so they could become parents. They had made discreet inquiries and eventually found a willing surrogate. Mary Beth Whitehead, a woman with sturdy blue-collar roots who had already borne two of her own children, had agreed to be artificially inseminated with William Stern's sperm and then surrender the child to the couple for $10,000.

However, after the child was born, after she had touched with her own hands the live flesh of her daughter, who had lain under her heart for nine months, after she had felt the child suckle at her breast, Mary Beth Whitehead changed her mind. The child was hers, she claimed, by all the laws of nature, and so one day she came to the home of the Sterns', made an impassioned cry from her heart, and took the baby away. The Sterns gave her the baby, claiming that they were afraid she would do herself some harm, and Mary Beth fled to Florida, dug in her heels, and gave back the money.

Like all good, upper-middle-class, law-abiding citizens, the Sterns went to court for their remedy. Even in that first reaction, there was a strong divergence in their behavior. The natural mother acted on impulse; the Sterns acted on rational grounds. They operated by intellect.

As the details accumulated, as the clouds of the storm began to take on some shape, those of us following the case in the offices of *A Current Affair* could see that this was no ordinary story. In my deepest night thoughts, I could sense that it was one of those compact modern parables that rose above the everyday chatter of events to make clear an elemental issue.

Artificial insemination. Surrogate parenting. The whole issue was fogged by technical advances. Whose child was it? Was the custody of a child just a matter of contract law, some technical question to be decided through civil litigation—the outcome buried in the fine print of a legal text? Should a child be sold in the marketplace? Where did motherhood begin? What rights did a father have? What about the interests of the child? In which home would the child flourish?

Never mind the question of genetic engineering and religion. Forget the cultural taboos. This was like the Scopes trial and the Lindbergh kidnapping all rolled into one. Mary Beth Whitehead had raised questions that had been simmering on the back burner of science and sociology ever since surrogate parenting had begun.

And we knew it. I don't know how, but some very exposed nerve had been touched with fire and we were suddenly alert and after the story.

The characters themselves were almost perfectly cast for their roles. Mary Beth Whitehead was an attractive woman in an earthy, solid, frontier kind of way. She had a square jaw and exhibited a brave, stubborn pride in the way she stood her ground. It was that working-class streak of steel in her spine. You could picture someone like her planting a family on the plains and refusing to budge for Indians or tornadoes or government regulators—a mountain range of pride. Of course she was not fighting for anything trivial—she was battling for her child. There was some populist appeal in that young face already furrowed and shadowed by a future of nothing but trouble.

The Sterns, on the other hand, were not gifted with winning ways. They were proper, distant, and they would not bend for cheap sympathy. There was a thin-lipped New England kind of curtness to their demeanor as they ran through the hailstorm of the media cameras and questions. They sought their remedies with lawyers and courts, and so lost a round to the backlash against the privileged elite.

Elizabeth Stern, it was said, did not want to go through the ordeal of pregnancy and childbirth. She suffered from an illness which made it riskier, but the way some people began to report it, the real reason for choosing a surrogate was that bearing her own would be inconvenient. It would interfere with her career. She was a doctor.

On some high level of intelligence she understood that she could not compete with Mary Beth Whitehead for public sympathy. Mary Beth had too much going for her. And so Elizabeth Stern kept custody of her own ordeal, which was in many ways very admirable, very noble. However, silent, thin-lipped strength does not make for good television. The jury always wants to see the guy take the stand.

On the other hand, Mary Beth Whitehead was an American Gothic. She was a sturdy oak who represented the traditional family values and stood up against the family-engineering Philistines, which was, in this case, modern science and artificially constructed families. Her fight was an old one. She was trying to stop the collapse of American values, Western civilization. She stood for time and tradition and the history of the species.

Of course she had strayed from the fold when she had accepted the $10,000 fee to bear William Stern's child, but she had recovered and been brought back to her senses in time and was now a hot convert to the antisurrogate army. She preached natural families and natural motherhood and became the darling of American forgivers, who adore reformed sinners, especially when they confess their sins publicly. The fact that they have actually been inside the enemy camp and know first-hand the taste of sin adds a little spice and thrill to their rebirth.

And there was a crossover appeal. Feminists found in her a great heroine—a woman whose rights were being trampled by cruel, male-dominated custody laws. Hers was a wide banner; she was a symbol for the Right and for the Left.

In August of 1986 the Sterns sued to recover the child, whom the courts called "Baby M." Mary Beth had named her Sara, as if any more Biblical implications were necessary. That is where things stood when the court reporters got their hands on the motion papers, and short, crisp items began appearing in the newspapers. As the interest grew, so did the size of the articles and the stature of the coverage. Now, columnists and feature writers moved into the case and gave it the heft of thought and an artful rendition. Mary Beth Whitehead was lifted above a court case and given the stature and dignity of an American martyr. Positions were taken. A cause had been struck!

Maybe I didn't know what "our kind of story" was yet, but I knew something important was going on here. Brennan sensed it. Dunleavy sensed it. Like some high-pitched sound that only a dog hears, our ears perked up all at the same time. I knew that I had to get an interview with Mary Beth Whitehead. The story was bursting like sap. It was all anyone could talk about. All you had to do was listen to the women in the office, with their passionate opinions, their views that had hardened like cement, and the way they looked at men with that pitiless special knowledge, as if men didn't have any right to an opinion on this one.

An updated *Stella Dallas,* I told Brennan, who agreed. Our viewers—that great mass of as yet unidentified and unsuspecting good-hearted people—would weep at the good woman who could not afford to raise a child in the splendor that the Sterns could provide. The crowds were already trembling with sympathy and rage, which was exactly what we were after. The more I thought about it, the more I thought that this is what journalism had come to: politics and beliefs had already been decided in some visceral debate beyond our comprehension. Information only gave the public an excuse for their pre-formed beliefs. Maybe this was what journalism was supposed to do—act out something that had already been decided biologically or over the water cooler. Maybe *A Current Affair* was supposed to be a steam valve for the explosive pressure building all around us. It had nothing to do with intellect.

Everyone was trying for an interview with Mary Beth. So far all we had were the arid statements of lawyers and interest groups. We all wanted the emotional pop. I'd been in the business long enough to know what it was that made the ratings sing. We chased those rare moments when events happened spontaneously. The camera catching Mafia boss Frank Costello's guilty hands giving the game away during Senator Kefauver's crime hearings. The confrontation between Welch and McCarthy when that old jungle lion of a lawyer finally called the mischievous senator to task with his famous "Have you no shame, Senator? At long last, have you no shame?" The migrant's face. The cry of the victim. Such elusive things, so hard to find without the poison of being staged. Of course there were always the cooperative subjects, people so dazzled by the cameras, by television, that they would heighten the effect. Tears wept on cue. Women who lost children and granted interviews! Collaborators.

Not that any of this discouraged us. It made us a little cynical, and some people on my end of the microphone would encourage the "re-creations," because that's what they were. Even the parents of dead children would "re-create" their grief to be on television. It wasn't just fame seekers, it was to memorialize their dead, to exist, to make some lasting testament, as if television were an imprimatur, a headstone of all our lives.

No, we were not discouraged, just hungrier for the real thing. We worked harder to find the authentic emotion. In a strange way, people who turned down interviews, who played hard to get, became all the more desirable. They were not going to display artificial, "re-created" grief. They were harboring the real thing. Those were the ones we went after with everything we had. And Mary Beth Whitehead wanted no part of us.

I tried to convince Mary Beth and her cadre of lawyers and advisers that in spite of all available evidence *A Current Affair* was a legitimate and worthy news program. Of course I was only guessing. After all, I had actually witnessed those daffy story conferences in which the members of our crew pitched suggestions for shows that sounded like outtakes from the Marx Brothers. The rundown, on any given day, would include televangelist spoofs, tales of quadriplegic killers, reports of Satanic teenage murders, cow-mooing contests, Marilyn Monroe bulletins, Elvis sightings—all presented with a kind of wide-eyed exuberance by our goofy staff. They managed to make each farfetched shocker sound like a happy pop of a champagne cork. As the resident grown-up, I always felt like the bomb squad.

The ability to convince total strangers that I was all right was a powerful weapon, essential to any television journalist. I brought the gift of credibility and sincerity to the show, and it was this same gift that I used to try to convince the people surrounding Mary Beth Whitehead that her ordeal would best be depicted on a program like ours.

Her lawyer said he would have to think about it.

We all had to think about it. After all, why *should* she come on our program? What did we have to offer? Why should she pass up Koppel and Rather and all the rest of those sainted superstars to talk to us? We thought about it in the loud clutter of my office, with its carpet of magazines and newspapers, its batch of NFL footballs and standby golf clubs. We thought about it in the silent frenzy of Brennan's office, with the door closed and the phone off the hook and the television picture flickering soundlessly next to the big clock. We thought about it in those after-hour conferences at The Racing Club when we tried to help it along with liquid propellant.

"Peter," I said one day in desperation, "what do I do? What do I tell this lawyer?"

"Tell him we're different," said Brennan. He tilted back his head and let gravity do the work on the beer in his hand.

"I *know* that," I said. "But how? I mean—"

And then suddenly I realized he had put his finger on something. This was New York City, which exploded with attitude. There was no such thing as "too extravagant." Peter Brennan had given me one hell of an idea.

Turning to Brennan again, I said, "You know, I told that very same thing to the lawyer. Almost to the word. I said to him, 'We're different.' "

"Well, there you go, mate. That should have satisfied him."

I shook my head. "No. He said everybody claimed to be different. Every slaphappy talk clown says the same thing. And I know what he meant. All these reporters, held together by hair spray and Armani sports jackets and flashing Dentyne smiles. We look alike. We all sound alike. We're all trying for the same girl with the same line and the lawyer has heard it all. He doesn't believe that we're different."

"Well, sod the bastard."

"No. No. But we *are* different. It just hit me. You know *how* we're different?"

Brennan looked up and down the bar, as if the answer to my question lay in the accumulating stack of empty beer bottles at the many stations along the counter and at the tables, and the slowly fading members of the staff who had not yet gotten their second wind and were beginning to sag into their stools.

"How are we different? Let's hear it, mate."

"We're different because we can be unfair," I said triumphantly.

He blinked, and then a light went on in good old Brennan's eyes.

I spelled it out. "We don't have to give equal time. We don't have to be fair. We don't have to show balance and display our virtue and responsibility, whatever the hell that is. We can run wild and tell an unbalanced story."

I knew then, in a flash, that ours was the perfect show for Mary Beth Whitehead. The only show! We were the only show that could possibly be one-sided and distorted, which, in some cases, is the only way to present an issue. We could give only her side. The whole damn show. We wouldn't have to water it down with the usual he-said/she-said bullshit.

"Mate, are you suggesting that we turn over a goodly portion of public airtime to an unbalanced, one-sided, biased, emotionally wrenching story?"

"Right. Outright, flagrant bias."

"Display an opinion?"

"Weeping in the aisles."

"By George, I think you've got it."

I got the lawyer on the phone and told him what we had just figured out. I was eloquent. "Look," I said. "The trouble with modern journalism is that it has grown mathematically rigid. The people in charge of the ethical slide rules count the minutes and seconds. They have calculated that absolute fairness resides at some exact point equidistant between two opposing views. A meridian of truth. Not so. The truth can be somewhere else. Completely one-sided. And we do not have to be prisoners of that strict and silly system.

"That's why we're different. We're completely flexible. Mary Beth will own half an hour of major airtime. She can speak in tongues for all we care. Our show will belong totally, completely, to Mary Beth Whitehead. She will be able to present her case without interruption, without challenge, with only a sympathetic listener—me—to guide her along, so that she doesn't get bogged down. You are never going to get a better deal. Unless she comes across as a raving madwoman, millions and millions of Americans all across the land, coast to coast, will leap off of their couches, weeping and cheering for this underdog woman who only seeks her inherent right of motherhood."

Frankly, it was a very appealing pitch—and, what's more I believed it. On any other newscast Mary Beth Whitehead would be torn apart by those journalistic pit bulls who, in the name of balance, yapped and nipped at anyone in the public eye. We, on the other hand, were not going to dredge up the family's domestic problems: the husband's drinking, the breakups and fights. The whole checklist of underclass woes would be implicit but unreported. In other words we pledged to be her mouthpiece for twenty-one minutes.

I didn't tell him that we would use the exact same argument with the Sterns—and we would mean it. We did intend to be fair. Balance does not mean playing rhetorical Ping-Pong during a particular program. What was wrong with showing one side of an argument on one night, then showing the other side the next night? The rules do not force you to display both sides of an issue on the same show. You don't have to answer every charge and accusation instantly. It could wait. The arguments would not go away. After all, we were not potted plants.

The Sterns had valid arguments of their own. There was certainly another side. I could imagine the sorrow and disappointment of a childless couple who, at the very moment of fruition, just when they thought that they had their baby, suddenly had the child snatched away by the biological mother—a woman who, let's face it, was not entirely rational about the matter. And this was not an immaculate conception. William Stern was the true biological father, so he had rights of his own to assert. There was, to be sure, a reasonable and passionate counterpoint to be made to Mary Beth's high emotion, and we would have been happy to present them both, on succeeding nights.

Frankly, I could see no flaw in my argument. Mary Beth's lawyer listened to my pitch—and then gave me the same weary reply that I was getting sick of hearing: I'll get back to you, I'll think about it.

How could he pass this up?

Easy. He didn't believe me. He was like a father sending his daughter out on a date; he thought we'd say anything to get what we wanted. He didn't know we were different.

Then, suddenly, things changed. The case was due in court on Monday, August 17, 1986. On August 14, at eleven in the morning, Mary Beth's lawyer called me—one of those calls that vibrate with subtle undertones. No one was saying what he really meant. The true agenda lay under a defense perimeter of evasion. He asked about me, I asked about him, but I knew that something else was coming. I knew it because I had covered enough trials to be certain that the moment this case came before a judge, he or she would impose a gag order. I knew it because it was a case involving a child. The courts, in their vast and infinite piety, must always seem to be protecting the child from the harsh glare of reality. What they are really protecting, however, is their virtuous image. Nevertheless, a gag order would bar Mary Beth from talking to the press. This was her lawyer's last chance for going public.

He chatted for a moment, testing the water, feeling the temperature of my sympathies, which because of my nature were always warm, then said, very casually, as if the thought just popped into his head, right out of the blue, "Why don't you go down and see Mary Beth and she'll do the interview."

I didn't scream, but I did stand up. I'd been sitting down in my office, my legs crossed on top of the desk, and when he made this oh-so-casual suggestion to drop in for a visit, as if I might be in the neighborhood or just passing by and it was a social thing, I came to attention. My eyes widened and my voice grew strong. "Fine!" I said a little too loudly. I told him that I'd be down in a few hours, made a firm appointment for the interview, and hung up before he could change his mind. That's one of the rules of the game: don't give them a chance to change their mind.

The studio went on full alert. Everyone was mobilized for action. Associate producers dropped everything and stood by for orders. Brennan appeared in my doorway, smiling uproariously. The conspiracy between us was inexpressible.

Younger producers started making phone calls, finding out where the convenient film crews were that day, and began plotting ways of getting both me and them to south New

Jersey at the same time. A logistical train had to get moving.

At the time, Mary Beth and her family were living in Point Pleasant, a sleepy Jersey coastal town north of Atlantic City. I was in a studio on East 67th Street about 100 miles away. My notes and fragments of the story were scattered all over the desk and on the floor, which is pretty much how I operated—messy but informed. I knew that this was the moment to drop everything and move. "We need a chopper," I told Brennan. This was no time to dawdle over expenses. "Get one at the Sixty-first Street heliport! Get a cab in Point Pleasant. Get our film crew to meet me at Mary Beth's house. It will be faster if they drive, so get started."

Brennan's smile kept getting bigger.

We were on a war footing. Researchers dropped other stories and got to work to provide backup when I arrived at Point Pleasant. That night's program was ripped open and schedules altered. I began to hope for two programs at least, depending upon Mary Beth's ability to speak and our access to the Sterns. I got reporters working on the Sterns. I warned them to be careful—not let the cat out of the bag about our interview; that would come later, after we had Mary Beth on tape, but to begin to press a little harder so that the timing would come together.

I began to believe that it would. You plunge ahead on faith and things begin to fall into place.

It was heady stuff. When you are about to go after a hot story, a change takes place. The pace of everything increases and the motions become, on the surface, slightly hysterical. I tried to act cool, but I could not hide the rush. I duplicated a lot of instructions because my mind was a blur and it was better to repeat myself than leave things out. My mind was already aboard the chopper, already down in South Jersey, already

smoothing the wrinkles out of my slacks and making Mary
Beth feel at ease so that she would open up to me on camera.
It was past noon and I was worried about the light. In some
intuitive way I knew that she had to be shot in natural light.
I was racing to catch the light, trying to hold back the sun.

Naturally, I knew that the final decision to be interviewed
on television hadn't come from the lawyer. He was too circum-
spect and timid and bound by court decorum for such a bold
move. The decision had to have come from the mother herself.
A few days earlier I had spoken—briefly—with Mary Beth
Whitehead and I knew the kind of stuff that she was made of
and that she had the last word in her world. Of all of them—
lawyers, cops, reporters—she was the one who had the spittle
to defy the courts and her husband, and heaven itself if it came
to that. She was a potent woman. I could tell, even from those
few moments on the phone, that she had been the one to come
to the conclusion that it was in her best interest to appear on
television.

In spite of the fact that I had conducted the important
negotiations with the lawyer, made the arrangements
obliquely, I knew, too, that I had entered into a kind of conspiracy with Mary Beth Whitehead. She had made a calculated
decision and I had been handy, but if it had not been me it
would have been someone else. We were doing this thing
together, and it was a little frightening.

The heliport was less than a mile from the studio, the pilot
was waiting, the engine was hot, and I strapped myself in the
seat and felt that jolting liftoff that reminded me, as if I needed
any more adrenaline, of the urgency of my mission. The East
River shivered underneath, and the bridge crossings to Brook-

lyn and New Jersey seemed as fragile as balsawood models. There was a certain amount of business to attend to during the flight, and I had my legal yellow pad in my lap: I had to organize my thoughts, remember the open questions that had to be answered. Above all, I had to devise a strategy for dealing with this interview.

First, and perhaps most important, I had to set the right tone. I would have to be tender and compassionate, for even in the worst case, if she turned out to be a crazy, I could not be cruel. However, there had to be some signal so that the audience knew I was not her prisoner. Even if I was sympathetic, there had to be some distance, some tiny, though perceivable, barricade between us so that the audience would accept me as an honest witness. They too needed a shield behind which they could take shelter, no matter which way it turned out. It was a tricky position to be in. I would need sharp backup questions. I would have to think of alternatives.

And I would have to make provisions for one other possibility: I would have to be ready in case she froze. There are people who, the instant that they get in front of a camera, become startled deer. They open their mouths and nothing comes out. They blink. The pores on their heads open up and they sweat like faucets. But no words. In such cases, you are obliged to carry the load. She could sit there wearing a glassy smile and I would narrate the story.

The helicopter pilot was busy chewing gum and engaged in businesslike ground chatter with air traffic controllers in Newark and in various traffic center control points. We were passing restricted airspace, watching Newark jets struggle up vertically so as to avoid outgoing traffic coming out of La Guardia and JFK, but the chopper pilot was in a protected corridor, sure of himself, and I envied his lighthearted, professional insouciance. He flipped switches and checked gauges and rattled on with the people on the ground in an offhand, easy style. He looked around, making certain that no one was moving into our airspace. He smiled at me, behind his pilot's sunglasses, relaxed and competent in the air.

On television we always fly blind.

Soon we were past the crowded air around the New York City and Newark airports, flying off the coast, but within sight of land, passing the motorists whipping down the highways. One of those cars had my crew and I looked for a moment to see if I could spot it. It was a silly thing, really. You couldn't spot a single crew, but it was quite human to look, all the same. When my father was in the Pacific as a war correspondent, my mother looked at every soldier's face. You never know.

Then I focused on the story. I knew that I was beginning with a distinct disadvantage. Mary Beth Whitehead didn't know me. I wasn't Walter Cronkite, or even Dan Rather, so it would take some time to woo her, to convince her that it was safe to unburden herself to me, a tall, salt-and-pepper-haired character with only common sense to recommend him. I had to show her that I was safe, because any normal person carries grave reservations about the utter finality of television's awesome first impression.

The rotors thumped and I could feel the pressure in my head. It was past two and I hadn't had lunch—not that I could have kept it down—and I watched the sun, as if I could stare it into overtime. These things take time to set up and I knew the timing would be close. I would see her children and ask about them, because a mother softens when you ask about her children.

By now I knew a lot more about Mary Beth Whitehead than when the case had first popped up. I knew that her own daughter, Tuesday, was ten, and that Tuesday regarded the disputed Sara as her true sister. I knew that Ryan was four and that he was confused, as any four-year-old would be, by the huge amount of fuss over this squalling four-month-old infant he regarded as nothing more than a mess of trouble. I knew all this because I had spent some time talking to the lawyer and to the people who knew her, and they had let slip revealing facts about the nature of Mary Beth Whitehead.

There was one other thing that I knew, and this was a television secret: There was a legitimate question which would make Mary Beth Whitehead cry. I knew it as a matter of certainty, because during my brief conversation with her, I had heard, far down in her throat, a sudden catch, a moist break in tone, whenever the subject was raised. I tucked the question away for the time being.

Brennan had promised the car would be waiting for me on the tarmac and the crew would be waiting at the Whitehead home, and they were. It was a plain house with no flowers or lawn to speak of, the sort of place rented for excess profit by absentee landlords. The Whiteheads stood outside, their faces twisted into forced, terrified smiles. There was Mary Beth, her sister and her husband—a gloomy man with a slouch—her son Ryan and her daughter, Tuesday. They looked at me, with my bright, salesman smile, as if I were coming to repossess the furniture. I kept the conversation low-key, drank the iced tea that was offered, loosened my tie, and admired the simple things inside the house.

We could have shot the interview indoors, but it was not what I wanted. We had flown in over the coast and I was struck by the appealing landscape, the great, open bay with the pleasure boats and the working fishing boats making their way through the channel and into their slips. There was the expanse of undeveloped land and the sense of windblown freedom, which I saw as a nice metaphorical background to the story: a woman's wild, natural instincts asserted in a powerful natural setting. I told her that it would look better if we could be filmed walking on the beach or near the marinas, because I already had the picture in my mind—her black hair blowing in the wind, the sky blending into the ocean, the grass growing wild, and Mary Beth Whitehead, unbroken and proud, bent forward.

She was receptive. More than that, she understood exactly what I wanted. We walked along the beach, through the high grass, and the crew took pictures from a distance and then up close. We might have been Kennedys walking along the beach at Hyannisport. She wore a blouse with thunderbolts across the front and that sad, flat smile that seemed a combination of sorrow and all-too-much knowing. She seemed friendly and leaned over in my direction to listen, as we talked about the baby and her passion. But I could sense something that the camera would catch as well: this was a troubled woman of endless woe. The camera panned down and there, at her side, was ten-year-old Tuesday, a grown-up child who had to carry more than her share of the load. She was there for ballast, and she kept her mother from going overboard, the girl's pinched, suspicious eyes squinting out at the world.

We paused and stood on a dock, the pleasure boats behind us, and Mary Beth told her story, pushing the hair out of her eyes, a slight gesture, but somehow poignant, as if she hadn't enough to fight off without this, too. She spoke clearly and seemingly without emotion, but there was a strong undercurrent that was unmistakable. "It was my body!" she said over and over—a kind of incantation—and I knew this woman could ruin you in a fight. She had sustained so much loss in her young life, so many injustices, that, having picked this issue, she would go down scratching and kicking.

She had changed her mind, she said, shrugging off all other claims with a hint of mysticism. "This is why God gives you nine months," she said.

During the interview she tried to say some nice things about the Sterns, who were in hiding with the baby and unavailable for comment, but as far as she was concerned, they were only another oppressive factor in her melancholy life. They didn't even exist, except as justifications for her. "They came in and tried to take my baby," she said in that stone-cold tone of hers that seemed to explain everything, every kind of retribution. Yes, she felt bad for them and their nine months of anticipation, but it was her body and her baby!

She called Elizabeth Stern "Betsy," to demonstrate the intimacy of their relationship and to show that she was not simply a stranger who had come in and snatched a child. She said that "Betsy" had forced her to take a lot of unnecessary tests during the pregnancy. It is not cruel to note that she was intuitively aware of what she was doing and how to do it. She would express her sympathy for the Sterns, then grow hard.

She said that the Sterns were overbearing and cold, and turned for confirmation to her daughter, Tuesday, who frowned and agreed with her mother. The Sterns had reclaimed Sara on a day when Tuesday was alone, babysitting. Acting on orders of the court, police and social workers had come in and taken the baby. Tuesday had screamed and chased after them, hitting them with a hairbrush, claiming that they were taking her sister. As far as Tuesday knew, the Sterns had sent these people to her home and taken Sara from her crib, fracturing the family in the process.

The tragedy, however, was already waiting to happen. At

the time, no one knew how badly broken the Whitehead family already was. No one knew about the separations and the drinking and the financial struggle. We stood there and talked about primal needs—a baby who belonged to its mother. In the background the boats inched by, and birds swooped low and the grass swayed in the wind.

We got along well. I saw Mary Beth's pain, and if I didn't understand the depth or the meaning, I recognized her wound and she was grateful for that. I stumbled on one or two questions, mispronouncing words, but that didn't bother me. It lent an air of unfinished reality and a certain amount of raw credibility to the interview. And then, eighteen minutes into the broadcast, I asked my question:

"What happens if you don't wind up with that baby?"

It didn't open her up like a knife. The tears were subtle, tucked behind that brave smile. She had been waiting for the question.

"It's gonna hurt," she said. The smile stiffened and the tears fell more quickly. She blinked and there was nowhere else to look, and she added, with a small sob: "At least she'll know we tried."

If it sounds hard and cynical, it wasn't. Mary Beth knew by all that we learn from watching television that she had to cry. Mothers cry. If she remained unmoved, it would have left a gap in the story, a doubt about her mother's heart. She knew that I had to ask the question and that the thought of the loss of the baby would bring the tears. I was merely her surrogate audience—the real audience was public opinion, and the pressure it would bring to bear on the court.

Cora-Ann Mihalik, one of our reporters, anchored the show on August 14, explaining that I was down on the Jersey Shore, where I had just gotten an exclusive interview with Mary Beth

Whitehead. Cora-Ann tried to display an evenhanded attitude about the program and the issue, but without the Sterns and with only Mary Beth and that poor, overburdened child, Tuesday, it was no contest. Sympathy oozed out of her like sap.

Later, back at the studio, some tone-deaf technician complained about the background noises—the boats and the birds. He carped about the wind blowing the hair in her face and all that effort she had to make to hold it back, which, according to this technician, interfered with the smooth, unimpeded interview of the mother and daughter. I started to get up on my haunches, ready to explode, because all those things gave the story texture, heft, a sense that we were there, out in the open, contending with a force of nature itself.

But I didn't have to bother, because Peter said gently, "It's fine, leave it alone, mate," and I knew that he understood.

We had our story and we had done it our way. Or, Mary Beth's way. I still don't know.

We never did get the Sterns on the air, even though we tried. They never wavered in their belief that the news media should be ignored. Very rarely does a major player in a news event continue to shun the microphone, but the Sterns did and still do. The pressure on them seemed unbearable. I have great respect for their silence.

A week later John Corry reviewed the show in the *New York Times*. After all that groping and strain, he told us what we were. "*A Current Affair* is tabloid journalism. Forget now the pejorative notions that cling to the phrase; *A Current Affair* is tabloid journalism at its best. It is zippy and knowledgeable, and when it falls on its face, at least it's in there trying. The new weeknight series, on Channel 5 at 11:30, is the equivalent of a good afternoon newspaper. . . ."

I could have wept. All my life I'd been groping for some clear definition of my style of journalism and now I had it. I was an afternoon tabloid, full of blood and gore and happy mischief. Full of life. I wanted to sing.

Rupert was similarly moved. He changed us from eleven-thirty to seven-thirty, in the process knocking out one of the station's biggest money-makers, "M*A*S*H" reruns. We were on the lip of prime time.

The business people were shocked and in an uproar, but Rupert understood the implications of the rave review in the *New York Times*. It changed everything. I thought it was nice, having a good review in the *Times,* the good gray lady of journalism. It would give me points with my friends and my family, it would bestow respect upon the show and extend my credibility. But I had no idea of the reach—the long and far depths of the impact in the financial community, where respect and a little sex appeal mean big bucks in advertising.

And there was the cultural wallop carried by the *New York Times.* We were no longer that vulgar show you had to hide between the covers of the real news. According to the *Times,* we were strictly kosher.

Chapter
Eight

I can't tell you how good that made me feel. After all that time I had spent in the wilderness—to be recognized. The "lost years" reared their head again. I felt I could face them now.

I've said that back in the seventies, I experienced a kind of emotional crash, and that's exactly what it was. I felt it first after Nixon and the Watergate years, when Gerald Ford, a nice enough man, issued the vile pardon. I was deflated. All that Watergate effort for nothing! All those hearings and that proof, squeezed out like labor pain, all those daily arguments that had ended up in sputtering rage, and now it ended with a whimper! I took it very personally. I shouldn't have, but I did.

I was also bored and restless, personally, professionally, every which way. I lost my interest in *Panorama* and spent time doing shows on *est,* poking fun at Shirley MacLaine and Werner Erhard, getting my jollies off at everyone, because in 1975 and 1976, there was no action in America. I was in my mid-thirties, working seven days a week, and the networks had not called. As far I as I could tell, they were never going to call. I was a local star, but it was not good enough. I interviewed Sevareid and Rather when books by them came out, and a nasty little worm of envy ate itself into my heart. I was doing things that these high-paid anchors were not doing, I felt—asking hard questions on vast issues, virtually grabbing John Dean by the throat—but completely unrecognized by the networks. As far as they were concerned, I was a loose cannon, a man with an inflammatory, confrontational style. Not their kind of guy.

It got so bad that I extended it to the public. I blamed the people of Washington for not appreciating me. And then one day I went on the air and acknowledged my indisputably ragged appearance and bloodshot eyes with a simple explanation: "Fact is," I told the audience, "I'm a little hung over." It was amazing how many people took that openhearted display of candor badly.

And so I decided to move to another town, a place where no one would know me and I would make my mark. In a moment of infantile, self-destructive anger, I went to my own station and demanded a whopping raise from $75,000 to $100,000 and when they naturally said no, because no one got that kind of money on a local station in Washington those days, I called my agent, Alfred Geller, and told him to get me out of there. The stipulation I gave to Geller was that wherever I went, it had to be owned and operated by a network. I wanted a network to have a good look at me. He called my bluff. NBC in Chicago needed a news anchor.

Thus began my long odyssey.

On the second day of January in 1977 I reported for work in the city of big shoulders, and when I picked up the *Chicago Sun-Times* and the TV reporter wrote: "Here comes another anchor who doesn't know how to pronounce Chicago," I thought to myself, boy, you really do need big shoulders in this town.

I was working with a guy named Ron Hunter, who reminded me a bit of Ted Baxter. He would only show one side of his face to the camera, and he would angle that part so you could see only one eye. He even had a secretary, and no one I knew in the business had a secretary. Ron did not go out on stories. Period. He had his anchor seat and there he stayed, anchored. Later, he would show up on *A Current Affair*, himself the subject of a very shocking story, and one that would have a significant effect on my own career.

But at the time, I was fighting for my life and I went out and covered stories. This was a town of killer competition— murders, rapes, fires. Everybody was out, wearing out their shoes, fighting for their lives. This is where I learned that reporters swipe pictures off the mantelpiece as a matter of course.

I had drinking buddies who worked on the newspapers, and there was one ugly murder and rape to a Baptist family that had moved up to Chicago from Oklahoma. One of my buddies, a Pulitzer Prize–winning reporter, and I were together at the funeral and afterward, and we didn't get near any of the people, or at least I didn't think that we did. Later, though, I picked up the newspaper and there was a great story about the family with my drinking buddy's by-line. I ran into him that night at our drinking hole, O'Rourke's, and said, "How did you do that?"

He said, "Well, I talked to the mother and I showed her my sympathy and she asked me how I understood all of this, and I told her that my father was a Baptist minister from Oklahoma, and she just opened up for me."

I was impressed. We had a few more drinks and were walking back to my car when I said, "I didn't know that you were from Oklahoma."

And he said, "I'm not."

"I didn't know that you were a Baptist."

And he said, "I'm not."

"I didn't know that your father was a minister."

And he said, "He's not."

I looked at him and he was smiling, and I said, "So that's how they play the game in Chicago."

Soon after I got to Chicago, there was a bad accident on the el. Two trains collided forty feet in the air, above the streets. There were cars dangling, people killed, fire and rescue units all over the place. I ended up anchoring the special report, and I have to say, I was pretty good at it. It's not an easy thing to do, to sit there with people yelling in an earpiece, describing raw tape as you're seeing it for the first time, switching from reporter to reporter and balancing everything live. But then I have always said that anchors earn their pay only ten times a year. Some people have the knack for it and some don't.

After that I began to feel comfortable, to think that Chicago was really going to work for me. The town was great—wide open, no-holds-barred, open all night—a big drinking and brawling town.

My family came out in June and we bought an apartment on the lake and everything seemed fine. The only thing bothering me was that after six months they had still not signed my contract at the station. Then one day the station manager came to me and said, "You're doing noon news." I did not want to do the noon news. The evening news was fine by me, and if I had had a signed contract, that contract would have said no noon news. I especially did not want to do it under duress, but the situation soon degenerated into his telling me, "You'll do what I tell you to do," and my telling him, "Oh, no, I won't," and before I knew it I'd said, "I quit," and they'd threatened to sue me. My brother, David, the high-powered Washington attorney, rode to my rescue. NBC never sued. When I left, it was on the front page of the *Chicago Sun-Times:* "Povich leaves!"

I called Alfred Geller again and told him to find me another job, and he came up with Los Angeles. That was a CBS station. All that shifting and moving began to have a corrosive effect on my family. Phyllis said that she would not move again, not after pulling the kids out of school and planting them in private schools in Chicago. She said I should go to California and come back to visit on weekends, and we agreed that we should try it. In Los Angeles I anchored the news with a woman named Connie Chung. She had moved up the ladder very quickly, with great determination, and I had nothing but the highest opinion of her.

The trouble was Los Angeles itself. I had just come out of a frontier world with newspaper gunslingers on every corner and *Front Page* competition between reporters, and all I could think of was Fred Allen's description of the coast: "California is great if you're an orange."

Nobody cared about television in Los Angeles. Nobody wrote about it in the newspapers. It was just there, like smog. In Chicago, everybody was inside watching television news. In Los Angeles, they were in their cars listening to the radio, or beaching it. Different cultures, different tunes.

I spent a month in the Beverly Hills Hotel and then rented a house in the Hollywood Hills. The station ran a promotion, "Who is Maury Povich?" only it backfired because nobody knew and nobody cared. They'd run a dumb promotion in Chicago, as well, with Hubert Humphrey and Eugene McCarthy endorsing me. Nobody cared about that, either—in fact they'd resented it because Humphrey and McCarthy were considered outsiders: what did Chicago care about two Minnesotans?

The first night in Los Angeles I was very nervous and thought the show went badly, and Dick Goldberg, my producer, said, "Cheer up!" and took me to The Palm. It was a famous restaurant with great food, and some of the help knew me from Washington. After a few glasses of wine I felt a little better. Then I went to the men's room. One of the walls had a blackboard on which people were supposed to write clever things, and someone had scrawled, "Maury Povich sucks!"

Welcome to L.A.

The station was fifth in a three-station market. It was bad. Very bad. Connie was the only strong thing they had going for them, and even she couldn't save it. I couldn't figure it out. You couldn't go out and chase fires or shootings. In L.A. the news was so laid back that it hardly existed. Every single star on the Hollywood Walk of Fame made it onto the newscast. If Red Buttons was going to get a star, we did a package with a reporter and sound bites and clips.

Even if it didn't have the teeth of Chicago news, though, it wasn't all soft. The Roman Polanski story was big then—he'd been charged with the statutory rape of a fourteen-year-old girl and had fled the country. And there were a lot of water stories in Los Angeles: the droughts and fires and mud slides. You could tell the time of year by the type of story: June and July, we had drought; landslides were in January and February.

What I didn't know, or blinded myself to, was the corporate politics. I had always thought that my talent spoke for itself and that I did not have to play boardroom games. I was wrong. My hiring was the last gasp of a dying management. They wanted me to help save the ratings, as well as their jobs, but it didn't work that way, and a new management came on board and brought in their own guys. That's the way it goes. One day in walked a roly-poly guy with a beard, named Van Gordon Sauter, and in the beginning he was very friendly, told me not to worry and that I was his kind of journalist. He seemed very new wave and hip. I did not see the dorsal fin until it was too late.

There was one amusing story from that time. In December of that first year I went down to Mexico and did a few stories about jail conditions. If you had money, you could live like a king in a Mexican jail. If you were broke, they treated you like dirt. It was a good series, and it turned up on the CBS Morning News. I wanted to do a contrast, to show how we treated Mexican prisoners, so I went to an American jail called Lompoc. And there, just coming off the tennis courts, wearing a very nice tennis sweater, I saw a prisoner with a familiar face. It was Bob Haldeman. He knew me from the White House years when I'd hosted *Panorama*. We chatted for a while, and then I asked if he wanted to talk on camera, and he said, "No!" and "No pictures!" He sounded like the White House Haldeman of old who had issued dictates and decrees, and I had to smile at the leopard's old spots.

My personal life was again fading. I was going back to Chicago less and less, and in the beginning of 1978, Phyllis saw things more clearly and was, as always, more decisive: "This is not working out, and I think we should end it."

Naturally, she was right, but we'd been married for fifteen years, and Susan was fourteen and Amy had just turned eleven.

I was racked by what this would do to them. I told them, as gently as I could, but it would remain an open wound. It always does. And that didn't end it. I also had to tell my parents and I truly dreaded that. I kept putting it off.

One day in late March, Gordon Sauter called me into his office and said he had to make a change. I sat there, dumb, unable to grasp it. I was the change.

I suppose that I should have seen it coming. Geller had warned me that things weren't working out at the station, but I hadn't realized how far gone things were. I heard them, with their station chatter: "This is a tough thing to do, Maury. It's no reflection on you. I've just gotta make some changes."

I looked at him, feeling drained and pale, and asked for one favor.

"Anything," he said.

"If I could just have full use of the editing booth so I can get a résumé reel together."

It was funny in a very sobering way. I was thirty-nine years old. My family was breaking up, my job was kaput, and I made such a small squeak. The only thing I asked for was use of an editing booth. Not a big buyout. I didn't stage a big scene. I just absorbed this belly blow as if it were coming to me. Veterans had always told me, "Kid, you don't know this business until you've been fired," and I had replied, "Oh, yeah!" because I was a wise guy and thought I was immune. All those people I had seen over the years wandering the halls in a daze, I knew that they had just taken the same kind of hit.

Not long ago a young guy I knew got fired. He wasn't a drunk or a substance abuser or dangerously mental. He was just inconvenient. One day an executive editor woke up and had to make some budget cuts, and on that particular day the young guy stepped into the crosshairs. I saw him walking around the station, bewildered by what had befallen him. He was making audition tapes. Everyone else was rumpled and busy, but he was neat and fresh and all buttoned up. A dead man.

Later I would write Van Sauter that I had no hard feelings. The friendship was retrieved, slowly.

The day I got fired was the same day I decided to call my parents to break the bad news and the worse news. I was back in college, getting kicked out. My hands were shaking as I dialed the number. I could hear my father's speech about twisted values and broken promises. But when I got them on the line and explained the firing and divorce, my father came through for me.

"Son, I want you to do something," he said when I had told him everything.

"Yes?"

"I want you to take all of the sharp instruments out of the house."

For my father to say that, to couch it in humor, meant that he understood everything that I was going through. If he forgave me everything with that one quip, then I was reconciled with him forever.

"Why don't you come on home and we'll talk about it," he said.

I didn't. I lay down on the couch for a week and drowned myself in sorrow. I went to Chicago and saw my kids, and then I went to Washington.

After a while Ricki Gafney, a friend I'd known from *Panorama,* called. She was doing a morning talk show at an ABC station in San Francisco, called *AM San Francisco*, and they needed a male host as well as someone who could do the news. I went, and I could chalk up one more town on my national tour. By this point my friends were joking that I was indeed going network—city by city. San Francisco is a beautiful city, and in the summer of 1978 it shimmered. I was pulling down a decent salary doing the talk show and co-anchoring the news, but I remained in debt—my usual financial address.

In the beginning it was terrific. San Francisco watched television, and the people were nicer than in Los Angeles, but it was a small town. The lead anchor hated me because he was a "happy talk" guy and I wasn't. They wanted to lead the newscast with bizarre stories, such as a two-headed goat being born at the zoo or a guy getting his penis cut off by a train.

I began to make my mark, though. There was a big gas crisis at the time, and, feeling very cocky, I went out to cover the story. I found scandals in which some service stations opened at night for special customers, and the reporters at ABC began to accept me as a genuine, proven reporter, someone who was not afraid to go out and get dirty covering a story. Not long after that came the assassination of Harvey Milk and Mayor George Moscone in City Hall.

I spent two years in San Francisco, but I was drinking too much, partying too much, and generally living very close to the edge. Phyllis had remarried, and I was just filling up time. In my blind indifference I did not notice the dangerous political realignments at the station. The manager, Ross Coughlin, an ally, left, another came in, and I was told that they would keep me for the talk show but not the news. I had my usual reactive flinch: "No news, no work."

Which is how I wound up in Philadelphia, working for a Westinghouse station, an NBC affiliate. It was the middle of 1980 and I was treading water, all identity gone. I was a hard-news reporter, a talk show host, and a news anchor. Philadelphia was great. I'd gone to school there twenty years earlier, and I knew the town and loved the restaurants and loved the honesty. It was a town that contained both Frank Rizzo and Wilson Goode, and was willing to accommodate them both. A good place.

I was dating Connie Chung, but it was long distance. She was in Los Angeles and I was twenty-five hundred miles away, and we had to meet halfway in Kansas. But there was that sweet aspect of my life now, this woman with brains and charm and ambition, and I knew that something important lay ahead for us. I didn't think about it, because we were both so preoccupied with our careers, but like the success in my career, I knew that an unspoken future was out there for us.

We took vacations together. We met discreetly, and gradually I felt safe with her. She knew me and she knew the business and we could confide in each other in a way civilians could never understand.

Then, as happens so often in television—as had happened so often in my career—we got a new general manager. He held anchoring seminars in which he told me I was very bad and then he told me why. He said that I was not a conformist, which was irritating to the viewers. He wanted me to be nicer on the air. I said, "You can only be nice if the story is nice; how can you be nice when the story is awful?" He wanted me to smile as I told stories about killings and drugs and tragedies.

"There's a way to do it," he said. "Cronkite is nice when he does those stories. You could be nice."

When my contract was up in 1983, he said I could host the talk show but not anchor the news. I had met my biggest fear, which is that I had glimpsed my limitations. I was never going to be a network anchor. I had managed to acquire a reputation as a troublemaker, although, as I saw it, I was fighting for my own integrity.

I called Bob Bennett, my first general manager in Washington, who had become the president of Metromedia, and had been a friend and ally all along, and we met at the Regency for a power breakfast. He said, "I want you to go back to Washington." I slumped in my chair and refused. It was too much of a defeat. He was persistent. Go back to Washington, he said, host *Panorama* and anchor the news. The city'd welcome me back.

"The station has fallen on terrible times," he said. "Everything we created has gone. It's sagged badly and we need you."

This was the only guy who had ever given me a raise without my asking for it. He was the only one who had given me references and defended me. He was the only one I could trust.

And there was one more killer argument. At least in Washington they wouldn't have to ask who Maury Povich was.

And so I went home.

Chapter
Nine

BOB Bennett was right—the city took me back with open arms. *Panorama* soared, I soared with it, and the rest of my life seemed mapped out—until that fateful June morning when Rupert Murdoch's minions called me on the phone.

Now here I was on this kamikaze show, surrounded by madmen, inventing a new kind of television. "Tabloid journalism at its best," said the good gray *Times*. "Zippy and knowledgeable," they praised. I couldn't believe it. I was a hit—*we* were a hit. And it didn't stop there.

The summer of 1986 was a subtle milepost for television journalism. It was not the launch of *A Current Affair* that made it such an unusual season, but rather a dramatic shift in the technology and the climate of the art, which revealed itself on our show. The proliferation of home videos had become as common as family snapshots. It was in its own quiet way a revolution in the business of "reality" programming. We were quick to see the uses of such handy visuals, and when we went out on stories, we asked for them routinely, as we did in the old newspaper days when we cajoled or stole still portraits of crime victims. Eventually, the "Preppy Murder Case" would make the importance of this sudden flood of home videos clear to everyone.

It began on an ordinary Tuesday, the 26th of August, two weeks after our breakthrough broadcast with Mary Beth Whitehead. I had come to work as usual, and when I stepped off the elevator I could feel a jolt of something wild in the air. A strong story had blown our way and sent the staff into full alert. They were running back and forth like bees in a hive that had been disturbed. Steve Dunleavy, the man we called "the night prowler," had that intense, fierce look of a dog on the scent. Something serious was taking place.

Brennan was waving to me, motioning to get into his office. He closed the door and stood there for a moment and said soberly, "We got a call, mate. About a murder."

There were fifteen hundred homicides in New York every year. One more wasn't going to jump-start my engine. But Brennan was flushed and wide-eyed about this one. He said, "Jack Dorrian called Dunleavy with the tip."

Dorrian and Dunleavy were old "war" buddies, veterans of the night. They came out of the same rough-as-guts, working-class fortress and were sworn enemies of the British empire. They both had mutinous IRA hearts that remained unquiet in middle age, and they went way back together. Dorrian had once had another saloon down near the *Post,* where the reporters had drunk and hung out and told improbable inside stories about the world. His father before him had had one in mid-town, where Walter Winchell had had his own table and the romance of the business almost came with the territory. Dunleavy and Dorrian took pride in being second-generation, insubordinate, journalist rebel bastards. If there was a breaking story, Jack Dorrian would naturally call his old pal Dunleavy. And if he vouched for its size and quality, we could count on it, because he'd been around the business long enough to know the difference between smoke and fire; he was somewhere between a civilian and a journalist. In this case, he was more like a participant. He was an important player in the story.

Dorrian provided a few sketchy details for Dunleavy. In the early-morning hours of that Tuesday in late August, an eighteen-year-old girl named Jennifer Dawn Levin had celebrated a last fling before leaving for college in Boston. A pretty girl with a bubbling personality, Jennifer had left his bar—Dorrian's Red Hand—on Second Avenue near 84th Street about four-thirty in the morning on the arm of Robert Chambers, a heartbreakingly handsome youth who walked a thin line between respectability and crime and who had even managed to pile up a police record. His reckless nature thrilled all the impressionable girls of proper upbringing.

Jennifer had been found by a biker a few moments after six in the same morning in Central Park, behind the Metropolitan Museum of Art off the East Drive, near a grove of crabapple trees. Murdered. She was not technically naked; she was, however, profoundly violated. Her skirt was hiked up, exposing her belly and pubic region and her bare, bruised legs. Her blouse and bra had been pulled up and wrapped around her neck, leaving her breasts in the open. Her right fist was raised to the sky, as if in some futile rage at the heavens. She had been strangled to death with her own underwear.

The first conclusion by the police was that this had been the work of a psychopathic stranger. No friend or acquaintance would have left her like that, in an obscene heap. There would have been some regard for her dignity. In the experience of police, someone who knew her, even a murderer, would have protected her modesty. No, she had been taken to the park, raped, and strangled by a stranger. And so, to find the killer, the police tried to reconstruct her last moments, seeking witnesses who might have seen her being snatched off the street and forced into the park. That brought them back to Dorrian's, where she had spent the night table-hopping, in her coquettish, high-spirited fashion.

On the Monday night of the murder, the fill-in bartender had been John Zaccaro, Jr., the twenty-three-year-old son of the 1984 Democratic vice-presidential candidate, Geraldine Ferraro. Zaccaro was awaiting his own trial on charges of trafficking in cocaine as a student in Middlebury, Vermont. He had given Jennifer Levin her last glass of ice water, and he had noticed her in that dense crowd of rampant youth on a last summer binge because she had been so vivid and so happy to be alive. A hard person not to notice.

Dorrian's was, and is, one of those wood-and-glass pubs with gingham tablecloths, a working fireplace, and underage, upscale clientele. They were far too loud and far too rich and far too promiscuous for their own good. If you wanted to see what had become of the legacy of the political activists of the sixties and seventies, they were at Dorrian's, a generation flashing phony IDs and coolly indifferent to social concerns and global threats. The extent of their ecological concession was drinking diet soda. Their style was pleasure-driven and self-centered. The girls compared their sexual experiences and the boys made career moves.

The first moment I walked into the bar, later that night when we broadcast our program from there, I thought to myself that on a thousand bleary nights I had been inside a thousand such bars, where I had sat among countless suspendered yuppies and girls with raven hair. It was a familiar and chilling feeling. I had sat in the same kind of bar in Chicago and Los Angeles and San Francisco and Philadelphia. They were like airports, with their relentless sameness and predictable codes of behavior and depressing impersonal blinders. The artificial mood of clubby belonging, the deafening music to mask the impoverished conversation, and the unspoken and unmistakable signals of halfhearted acceptance and cruel rejection—it was always the same. Nothing meant anything. As I stepped through the door and was struck by the overwhelming knowledge that I was there because of a death, somehow I knew that the whole careless era was over. Casual sex and make-believe relationships had died along with poor Jennifer Levin. A turning point had been reached.

The story really appealed to Brennan, with its sinister taint of upper-class decadence. It exposed the worst inclinations of the American aristocracy. The outcast Australian egalitarian fanatic in him was really a social subversive, when you got right down to it. Brute upper-class insolence pushed his button.

Brennan leaned over to me and said, "It's a sensational story, mate. A classic. Rich kids getting into trouble. Prep school snots who own the Upper East Side and wind up murdered in the park. Marvelous."

Dunleavy was already on his way up to the bar to talk to Jack, who was scared silly, because he thought that he was about to be made the scapegoat for this crime. He had good reason to be afraid. The cops were already leaking innuendos about the history of the bar, that Dorrian's gatekeepers were notoriously lax and overlooked the fake IDs of the thirsty uppercrust. Dorrian had already been brought up before the State Liquor Authority about it, and his license was suspended for ten days. The media "take" on the story was that, in the absence of the killer, Dorrian was the villain, for corrupting innocent youth.

Our people didn't see it that way. The murder was not a temperance problem, but one of rank. We saw it as the inevitable outcome of the abuse of privilege. Jack Dorrian was a convenient substitute for our own parental neglect. To us, he was a working-class slob, a surrogate for the real vipers, who were always the ruling class.

We set up our equipment in the bar, pushing tables aside, running cables across the floor, adding a media thrill to the everyday shock of New York's Upper East Side. The program itself was a disaster technically. I sat at a table and watched as all of our equipment failed. The signal didn't get back to the studio. The sound was lost. The videos were scrambled. It was a true catastrophe. However, we laid down a foundation, establishing our presence, getting to know a number of the regulars and denizens of the neighborhood, making friends. The story on the first night was bad, way off base, but in a year or more, our sources and diligence would pay off, and we would have the best story of all.

That was another lesson I would learn on *A Current Affair:* patience. Dunleavy knew about it, because he had worked in newspapers and acted as if he didn't travel around with a crew. He spoke to people, and listened to them, and they could tell the difference. He kept in touch with people, he called back again and again and chatted with his sources. He listened to their complaints and sympathized with their troubles and asked what was new, and when something new did turn up, he was always among the first to know. It was that business about not knocking on the grass, but going all-out to cover a story. We were laying down bear traps for the winter, like mountain men.

And he was not the only one. They all burned late on our show. No one dogged it, and no one complained about the hours or the demands. Maybe they should have, but they didn't. They showed up earlier than anyone else and they stayed longer and it paid off, because we were not hotshot stars and the public took to us.

This was Raf's first story: Rafael Abramovitz, the mad monk who had been a civil rights lawyer before he had gotten bored and jumped into journalism, where he could display his hair shirt in a larger arena than a courtroom. He had been given a job as a producer on the show because everyone agreed that you couldn't put him on camera, not with that ponytail and that thick accent, a goulash of the eight European languages he spoke. But Brennan wanted him on the team. He liked the man's passion—a volcano that lurked just under the surface—and maybe he even admired the defiant ponytail and the ten-gallon hat and cowboy boots that seemed so out-of-place on this European Jew with so many grievances against society.

Brennan turned Raf loose with a crew, but while we were all at the bar, committing this atrocious live program, Raf tried something smart: he went to the park.

It was the logical move. Cops are creatures of habit, he told himself. They operate on schedule. If he went back to the park at the same hour as the body had been found, he would find the cops who had been on duty during that shift. He would also find the people who inhabited the park at such an hour, and maybe get lucky and dig up a witness.

He did indeed find the cops and talk to them, and they explained what the park was like at that hour, between midnight and dawn, when even the muggers were sleepy, and whom you could expect to see—and Raf was struck with a brilliant idea. He thought that Jennifer's story could be told through a re-creation. It wouldn't just be some reporter standing at the site and narrating, saying this happened at such-and-such a time, she was walking here when last seen alive, etcetera. He wanted to hire actors and put them in shadows, so you couldn't see their faces clearly, and show them going through the deed. It was quite a daring notion. Of course he would have to be certain of the sequence of events before he could attempt such a thing, but it was the seed of something. As a youth he had watched *You Are There,* in which historic events had been re-created, and he didn't see why it couldn't be done with more immediate events.

At the Arsenal Precinct on the transverse road, Raf went in wired. Under his thin necktie, he hid a microphone and some wires running to a transmitter. He told the crew to wait outside; he wanted to talk to the cop who had responded to the call, and he knew that the cop would freeze at the sight of a television crew. It was only when he went inside and stood before the high magistrate's desk where the lieutenant presided that he realized that he might get some feedback from the mike. If the cops were transmitting on the same frequency, they would get static, which would be followed by handcuffs and a Miranda Warning. Nevertheless, he was there and he found his cop and the cop spoke to him. The officer described the scene and spoke movingly about the emotions he had felt, seeing this attractive young girl who had been dragged into the brush and killed with her own bra.

Then Raf had come outside, proud of himself, boasting to

the crew, and the soundman had looked at him and asked, "Were we supposed to roll on that?" Raf sagged. They had recorded nothing. But he had his notes and a gritty determination, and he took the crew back inside and told them to stand on the side, shoot what they could, and record the damn interview. He grabbed the same cop and pulled him into the locker room and began going over his notes, making him repeat the same story—this time with the conversation being recorded.

The first thing Robert Chambers had done was lie. He had lied to his mother, and to the police, when homicide detectives came to his apartment on the top floor of a town house on East 90th Street off Fifth Avenue and questioned him about Jennifer Levin. Chambers admitted that he had walked out of Dorrian's with her, but he said that they had split up on the sidewalk. She'd been going off to meet another guy, her boyfriend, and he had grabbed some donuts and come home. This did not quite match the facts, since he had been seen walking with her, and so, after lying a little more, he said he had walked with her a little. The scratches on his face and hands, he said, had come from a cat.

"That cat better not be declawed," warned one of the detectives, and in fact it just proved what a lousy liar Robert Chambers was, because the cat did indeed have no claws.

He had given that same lame excuse to his mother, Phyllis, a woman with ambitions for her son. Divorced from her alcoholic husband, she worked as a private nurse to the powerful and wealthy, and wanted more than anything for Robert to move into the American aristocracy. She'd gone into debt to enroll him in private schools and pushed him into becoming an altar boy and joining gentlemen's clubs—and he had repaid her by flunking out of school and turning to burglaries to support his cocaine habit. His fleshy good looks—reminiscent of a young Elvis, with his full-lipped sneer—forgave him everything in her eyes.

His looks had the same anesthetizing effect on the young, Upper East Side debutantes who gazed into Robert Chambers' own ice-blue eyes. They thought that there was something romantic and exciting about someone on the fringe of their own set who had such an outlaw approach to life. In return, he had contempt for them. Robert Chambers blamed everyone but himself for all of his troubles. He called Jennifer "the bitch" for getting him into hot water.

When the police got him into an interrogation room at the Central Park Precinct, they dismantled his story piece by piece. After his alibi lay in shambles and there was nowhere left to retreat, he finally admitted that he had killed Jennifer Levin. But, he added quickly, it was her own fault. She had pursued him, lured him into the park, then viciously attacked him and scratched him when he had told her that he wasn't physically interested in her. He had, he said, been raped by the murdered girl. The detectives regarded this six-foot-four youth who claimed that he had been attacked and subdued by the five-foot-eight girl on that last, terrible morning of her life, and concluded that he would say anything to save himself. The cops came across people like that all the time. Criminals.

If that didn't convince them that there was something morally numb about Robert Chambers, what he had done after the murder cinched it. He admitted that he had watched the cops arrive and work on her body after she had been found. He had sat on a low brick wall across the road, and he had not moved as they had circled the area, roped it off and gathered up the evidence. He had been a bystander and he had spoken to a few other bystanders, asking them what had happened, as if he had simply wandered by. Then he had gone home. His only emotion had been curiosity, not remorse.

A curious thing happened after Chambers was arrested and charged with the killing. Jack Dorrian put up his bar as collateral to bail him out. Why? I can only conclude that he honestly believed the story. He truly bought the "rough sex" defense invented by the lawyer, Jack Litman, and hocked his joint to free the youth. There was another possibility, which was that he saw it as loyalty to his own class and Irish roots. Robert Chambers had sprung out of the working class and was Irish, and maybe that was enough to justify bail. In any case Chambers was soon free.

Our show was still running at eleven-thirty at night at the time and we were really cutting it fine. That first night we put on the first segment while we were still editing the second half, and it was a mess.

I was very unhappy with the program and determined that we follow it up and get it right. We went back again and again and talked to the kids and to the cops. Litman kept us dancing with his act. One day he said that he would get us an interview with Chambers, the next day it would vanish. He said that he was still working on it and I could sense that he was playing with us. He had no intention of delivering his client. I knew it for certain when *New York* magazine ran a cover story on Robert Chambers; Litman had delivered him to them, for a cover picture.

Raf wanted to do the re-creation. We were a little jittery, but Raf had good arguments. He brought up the Walter Cronkite precedent and said that he could do it in good taste. He would have it in black and white—separating it from the color segments of the show and giving it a grainy feel. And we would label it a "re-creation." He argued that it was a legitimate tool of journalism and should not be dismissed. We knew that we would take a beating from the critics, but that didn't bother us. We were inventing things as they came along all the time. This was really cutting new territory.

Brennan agreed, but he said that we had to research everything, down to the last button. In that sense it made us more thorough and responsible. We didn't want to catch criticism for little things, so we were very meticulous about the reporting. We blanketed the neighborhood and questioned the witnesses and talked to Litman and the prosecutor, Linda Fairstein, the sex crimes expert in the Manhattan District Attorney's office.

"Mate, make it economical," said Brennan.

And we did. The tone of it was low-keyed but powerful. Shadowy figures walked through the park, and the facts were recited off-screen, with the pictures of the real principals shown from time to time to remind the viewer that they were watching something that really happened.

Later, we would show them Robert's own re-creation and it would make our attempts look pale.

Chapter
Ten

WE weren't through with Robert Chambers. During the first year, as the case slowly wound its way to trial, we kept jabbing at the Chambers story, like a boxer waiting for an opening to land a knockout punch. We'd have an update or a new angle, reminding the viewers that we were still on the case. We assumed they knew the details by now, so we never went back to the top of the case; we just dropped in our new information and moved on. It gave us great flexibility.

Meanwhile there were a lot of other stories to cover. A style had emerged and the critics had taken notice. A few others, like the *Times*, got into the spirit and credited us for our juice and energy. Others dismissed us as checkout-counter fare. It didn't matter, because we were behind enemy lines and bursting with stories.

When you look back from the distance of success, it all

seems inevitable. In your memory, the accidents and quirks become acts of genius. It's not true, of course. *A Current Affair* didn't work out because we had a clockwork plan or a precision machine. The truth is that we were assembled by lucky hunches, good timing, and wild guesses—a haphazard outgrowth of people like Peter Brennan and whatever gods watch over idiots and TV wing-walkers. The public was bored and irritated with the usual style of covering the news. They wanted some hard advocacy, even if it did occasionally turn sloppy with sentimentality and rigid with indignation. There was also a vague feeling that stories were not finished when the package was presented. You couldn't end it with the arrest and trial of Robert Chambers. There was something else there, and we were after it.

But with all of that, it was the staff that made us so unusual and made the show work. We had Dunleavy, Miller, and Gordon Elliott, and an unlikely bench of players who could all hit it out of the park. They all wanted the seventeen-minute story. They were all hungry. Who could explain why it was that Brennan knew that Mary Hughes would turn out to be an important member of our team?

Mary was a young woman, just broaching thirty, when she came into the office, with a thin, pinched, ecclesiastical expression of unhappy reproach on her face. It was a beautiful face, in its hard-line way, but it was definitely unbending and judgmental in its outlook. How could it be otherwise? Mary was the culturally confused product of a strict Catholic and intellectually varied upbringing. She was an educated woman who was well read and well traveled, and spoke several languages, and dressed as if she had just stepped out of a convent: always in black, as if in a permanent state of mourning. She was the daughter of Emmet John Hughes, the late esteemed journalist and writer who had been widely regarded as one of the nation's keener minds.

In other words she belonged to an intellectual aristocracy— old traditions and high standards. How she would fit into our burlesque show, I had no idea, but Brennan saw something else. Sometimes I saw it too, a glint of mischief, a hint of a carnal smile. Sometimes you looked at her strict black wardrobe and thought, she must have some black-leather dresses in her closet at home. And the latent wicked streak showed itself at one strange moment.

During the late eighties, a small controversy broke out over nude bathing at a rocky beach in a small town on the Massachusetts border. The thing that made the story so hot was that the nude bathers—who had been using the beach for years— had to cross someone's property to reach the water. It turned out that the person was none other than George Shultz, who, at the time, was the Secretary of State under President Ronald Reagan. Shultz didn't really care about the nude bathers, but he was a high government official and it didn't really matter what he thought. It was a great story. So to whom did Brennan hand this hot potato? You got it. The immaculate virgin.

Mary and the crew drove up to Cummington, one of those New England towns on the Massachusetts/Vermont/Connecticut/New York border—a town filled with feisty New Englanders who had no complaints about nude bathers, if that's what people wanted to do, but had plenty to say about the press, poking into people's lives and privacy and bothering people about nonsense!

Mary spoke to townsfolk and got comments in that parched regional style.

"Do you know about the nude bathers?"

"Yup."

"Does it bother you?"

"Nope."

"What does bother you?"

"You folks."

She marched down to the beach—a rocky stream, really—
and the nude bathers turned their backs on her. They were so
mad that they got dressed. She was faced with coming back
with no story, a mortal sin in the catechism of our art, or with
taking the bull by the horns, so to speak. So she did what she
had to do. Our Mary Hughes—the immaculate reporter who,
we were certain, would swoon at the sight of naked bathers en
masse—disrobed down to her toes and plunged into the stream.
The crew, who were too bashful to follow her, started filming
as soon as she went for the first button. They got her sitting
on a rock in her altogether and trying to make the bathers feel
comfortable. Then she swam back to shore and started talking
to them. There she was, holding a microphone, buck naked,
while the bathers answered her questions, fully dressed in
protest.

Naturally, after she got back and edited the tape and we put
it on the air, everyone approached Ken Fuhr, her cameraman,
and asked what she looked like without clothing. To his credit,
Ken's lips were sealed. Mary Hughes' body drifted into fanta-
syland for the men at *A Current Affair*.

On the air, I said Mary had given us "the bare facts."

A year later Mary married J. B. Blunck. One of the original
producers of *A Current Affair*. I wonder if J.B. ever saw those
outtakes?

Brennan knew that Mary wouldn't let that story get away.
Faced with an empty spot on the air, she would do whatever
it took. Mary Hughes went all-out for the nude beach story,

a trifle, but she was also involved with a story about a Thalidomide baby who had grown to maturity with stunted arms and legs. The baby, named Maria, had come of age, learned to take care of herself, had a driver's license, and could cook, and it was clear that Mary's heart was in the story. She became, as they say, "involved." By conventional wisdom, journalists are not supposed to get involved in the story. They are supposed to remain objective and at some purifying distance.

But not us. We all had our passions. One day in the fall of 1986, David Lee Miller got a call from a woman on Staten Island. Her name was Celeste White and she told David that she had called *60 Minutes* and *20/20* and all the local stations, but she could not get past the interns. David Lee Miller took crank calls because he knew that one out of a hundred would be worthwhile. He panned for gold on the switchboard.

Celeste White had a frightening story. Her sister, Theresa Taylor, a former dental hygienist, had been murdered. She had been beaten to death by her husband, Dr. Kenneth Taylor, a dentist who was then serving a life sentence for the killing at Trenton State Prison in New Jersey. Theresa and Kenneth Taylor had a son, then two years old, named Philip Taylor. The custody of the child had been awarded to the dead woman's sister, Celeste White, after Dr. Taylor had gone to prison.

One day the paternal grandparents, Jean and Zachary Taylor, had come to visit and taken two-year-old Philip Taylor with them to their home in Marion, Indiana. Without telling the Indiana courts about the murder or the fact that the dead woman's sister had already legally adopted Philip, the grandparents applied for and were given adoptive status. It had all been engineered by Kenneth Taylor from his prison cell in Trenton.

David Lee Miller went to interview Kenneth Taylor at the

153

New Jersey prison, and it was clear from the tapes of that conversation that our fair and neutral reporter was smoking with outrage over what this guy had done. "Some people would question whether a convicted murderer should have anything to say about his child," he said at one point in the interview, and it was clear that by "some people," he meant David Lee Miller. The dentist looked at him long and hard—you could sense him containing his rage, and brave David Lee Miller let him steam, almost inviting an attack.

Then David jumped on a plane and was off to Indiana, where he ambushed the grandparents and posed questions like deadly arrows: Should they take custody of a child who had already been awarded to a family? Did they know that they were breaking the law and could be charged with a crime? The Taylors were plainly unaccustomed to such rough advocacy journalism and appeared rattled. David didn't care. He was on a mission. He had his teeth in the story. It was on our air four times in one year. We had lots of still photographs from the wedding album and private photos taken at home. One set of pictures had been taken on the honeymoon, when Dr. Taylor had been arrested by the Mexican police for beating his wife senseless in her hotel room in Acapulco. She claimed that she had been asleep and would not press charges. There were also long tapes of home videos, showing Theresa playing with her baby. That home video explosion was blowing up in Ken Taylor's face.

Finally the Indiana Supreme Court awarded custody to the sister, and David was there with film crews and private detectives. He rented two identical cars, Ford Tauruses, in case the Taylors tried to follow him or got an injunction to stop Philip from being returned to the Whites. He and Celeste and her husband, Jeff, took the child and drove to Dayton, Ohio, because it was the quickest way out of the state, and then they flew back to New York. You cannot watch that story and not feel the exploding indignation of our own reporter who, no matter what Rupert said about the Jimmy Chin story, had become a kind of cop. I'm very proud when I watch those tapes. This was not conventional journalism; it wasn't according to the lesson plans of the Columbia Journalism School. But it was something fine to see, the whole circle completed and the triumph of good.

Not that David didn't have his playful side. One morning in the winter of 1987, Jane Tomlin, one of our field producers, was driving to work from Westchester and heard a tiny little story, something we used to call "filler," about a sheriff in Kansas who had left a videotape in his rented camera when he had returned it to the store, after taping the amorous adventures of him and his wife in their bedroom. She came bursting into Brennan's office, where we were all sitting around. We didn't have meetings in those days; we had gatherings. People drifted in and out, and late at night they slept there, put together two or three chairs or maybe some boxes and camped out for the night. Brennan said he couldn't get a couch—it would be too dangerous.

It was a cracker-barrel gathering, and Jane told what she had heard on the radio and Brennan swept everything off his desk, took out a legal-sized pad, and wrote in very large letters: X-RATED SHERIFF. He formulated the promo first. Then he turned to one of the producers and said, "Get Miller."

They had two helicopters waiting to rush David to the airport. There were two cars at the Omaha airport, and a crew had come down from Chicago to meet him. David went into Council Grove, Kansas, and started asking questions, and it wasn't too long until the local constables were on his trail. He found out that most of the people in town had heard about the tapes even if they hadn't seen them. In the tapes, there was Sheriff Corky Woodward and his pretty wife, Danette, stripping for each other, fondling each other, and generally carrying on as if they weren't even married. David got some great interviews, the best being some old lady with blue hair he stopped at a supermarket. When David asked her what she thought of the tape, she paused and said, "Well, I'll tell you one thing, son—there ain't gonna be a Corky's Two."

David was at a pay phone talking to me and I heard him saying, "Oh, oh, Maury, they're coming down the street."

"Who?"

"The police. I can see the car. Here they come. They're coming for me now."

"David. Can you hear me?"

"Here they come, Maury, they're closing in . . ."

"David, just one thing: roll the camera. Did you hear me, David? Just roll the camera."

"They're stepping out of the cruiser and they're coming towards me now."

"David, we've already put out the ads on this one. We need the tape. It has to be on the air tonight. Make sure the camera is rolling!"

I was a little excited.

"Now they're arresting me . . ."

They took David down to the sheriff's office and there was Corky Woodward, the potbellied sheriff himself. He started asking what David was after, and David said he wanted an interview, and good old Corky groaned as he realized that he was not gonna be able to contain this story and so he gave David Lee Miller an off-camera interview. "Yeah," he said. "I left the tape in the machine when I returned it to the video store. I was under the assumption my wife took the tape out, and she was under the assumption that I took it out. When we couldn't find it, she thought I threw it away and I thought that she threw it away."

The folks in town just shook their heads at their clumsy sheriff. They weren't exactly put out about it, but they did resent the fact that he had gotten the town on the map in this particular fashion.

Mrs. Woodward, a cute little thing, said her momma had always said she coulda been a model. She seemed a little proud of her strip, part of which we showed on national television when David got a copy of the tape. I introduced the story on the air: "I think some of the best stories are the ones you say, 'There but for the grace of God go I . . .'"

A few weeks later Sheriff Corky got busted for drunken driving and was kicked out of office. Steve Dunleavy brought him to New York, put him and his wife up at a fancy hotel, and did another story about "The X-Rated Sheriff." There was a deeply human side to our stories. We liked Sheriff Corky, even if he had become the butt of a national joke.

And when we put the program on the air, we were not cruel.

Chapter
Eleven

IN October of 1987, fourteen months after Jennifer Levin had died in the shadow of Cleopatra's Needle in Central Park, Robert Emmett Chambers went on trial for her murder. His lawyer had been busy during the past year poisoning the wells against her. Robert Chambers was out on bail and staying at a church rectory, performing, so they said, good works. There were letters of support from Newark Archbishop Theodore McCarrick, an old friend of the Chambers family. He sang of Robert's virtues—claiming that the confessed killer possessed a "gentleness and a very special respect for people" reflecting an "unwillingness to cause pain."

This was in spite of the fact that he hadn't seen Robert Chambers in four or five years and was operating on the obsolete memory of a former angelic altar boy, not the callous cokehead who had in the meantime turned into a killer.

A defense fund was started by the Church, and money poured in. More than forty character references, mostly from Catholic-related groups, offered testimony on behalf of Robert Chambers. The extent of the Catholic mobilization struck some members of the public as beyond the bounds of Christian forbearance. It smacked of a warped bias. Where was the pity for Jennifer Levin? they asked, as the priests and monsignors allowed themselves to be placed conspicuously around Robert Chambers by the calculating defense attorney at the bail hearings.

Inevitably there was a backlash. John Cardinal O'Connor was so worried about the growing hostility between Catholics and Jews that he wrote a letter of condolence to the Levin family. And our own gossip queen, Cindy Adams, got an interview with Newark's Archbishop McCarrick in which he said he was having second thoughts about the letter of support he had written for Robert Chambers. He claimed that at the time he had written it he hadn't known about the drugs and the burglaries. Not that he still didn't offer guarded support for the youth.

Jack Litman, a Harvard Law School graduate, was not squeamish about the way he defended his client. He conducted a guerrilla campaign against the dead girl's reputation—something he'd done before in another case in which a youth had murdered his paramour. Litman dropped hints and rumors about a "sex diary" kept by Jennifer Levin, as if she had somehow plotted her own destruction and kept a lurid record of it which would place the blame where it properly belonged. It was an old tactic, shifting the blame to the victim. He planted stories favorable to his client in predictably sympathetic or pliable publications, selecting writers the way he placed the priests around Chambers in public.

He delayed the case as long as legally possible. Litman had been assistant district attorney in Robert Morgenthau's office—Linda Fairstein had served under him when she had graduated from Vassar—and understood in his bones that time was on his side. Witnesses grow wary or fuzzy, and to a jury the sheer distance from the crime creates a growing shadow of doubt about the accuracy with which the crime has been presented to them. Public indignation fades, but worst of all, the pictures of the dead girl are not as urgent or as sensual as the flesh-and-blood defendant with his aura of sorrow. No matter that the sorrow is for himself.

There was also the matter of the physical evidence. The jacket that Jennifer Levin had worn to the park and might have been an important part of the case disintegrated in the bins where the state's evidence was stored. The jacket had been wet when it had been tagged and put away, and Litman would have to have been a fool not to know what time would do to the fabric of the state's case. And the bantam lawyer was no fool.

Not that there was anything personal to it, but I wanted to get even with Jack Litman for the way he had manhandled us over the past year. He had promised interviews, then canceled, always claiming that he was doing his best to work things out. He had dangled the offer of an interview with Robert Chambers and kept us interested like a backup date. I told Raf that he would never deliver Chambers, and Raf smiled in that enigmatic way he had. I never knew if he was agreeing with me, recognizing something he had already known, or considered me a fool for ever thinking it was possible. Raf's like that: he keeps you nervous about your standing in his eyes. Dunleavy, on the other hand, was an optimist and always held out hope. "You never know, mate. You never know."

But I knew, and I told Brennan, and he nodded his head and

said that we still had to go after the story now that the trial was coming up. Raf would find some new way to do it, he said. Raf would come at it in some oblique and altogether postmodern fashion.

But Raf didn't want to do it.

"We've already done it to death," he said in that wheezy, tired whine of his.

"Do it one more time, mate," said Brennan.

Raf. Our saint. Touched with fire. He spoke of himself in the third person, as if you were not allowed to use his name in vain. But you needed such fiery prophets on a show to wander off in the wilderness and report back on our moral condition. By that time he'd cut off his ponytail and was an on-air reporter. Add up all his negatives and it did not hold a candle to the power of his righteous indignation.

Not that you could blame him. Raf had escaped one step ahead of the Nazis at the end of World War II, walking out of Poland in the middle of the night and entering Czechoslovakia clutching the hand of an uncle, following the patch of white sewn onto the coat of the man ahead. He always spelled his last name because it came out of such a deep graveyard of the past. The name meant "blessed by God," which Raf had come to take literally. There was significance in the first name, too. Rafael meant "healer," and he would tell you that as well, because he did not want to be misunderstood: he had work to do.

He spoke Czech, Swedish, Hungarian, Polish, French, Yiddish, Hebrew, German, and English. As a result, Raf was able to make his way in the world, a citizen of the worthy cause. In spite of all that turmoil and dislocation, America was the place he felt most at home. He thought of himself as a full-scale child of the American tradition, an admirer of the Revolution,

an advocate of the brillance of our Constitution, a weeper and
bleeding heart over the notions of liberty and equality. A seeker
of justice.

Who better to send after Robert Chambers?

Raf went out after the story and started hunting the Upper
East Side. He spoke to all the people we had spoken to before.
He rounded up the kids and he rounded up the parents and he
tracked down the cops and he was beginning to get the outlines
of a final, complete, everything-you-ever-wanted-to-know-
about-Jennifer-Levin re-creation.

Not that he was happy with it. He began attending the trial.
It was a long one. Jury selection alone took eight weeks. All
through that autumn and winter, the spectators lined up in
corridors to get a seat. They stood behind barricades and
waited, some holding bags of lunch, some holding newspapers,
some reading legal textbooks. There were the old-timers—the
buffs—who came to the trials as their theater. There were the
thrill seekers and the passersby who were just curious to see
what was what. And there were the kids. Raf knew a lot of
them from the first stories. They would cluster together in
their various rooting packs. A few were there in a kind of vigil,
to pay respects to Jennifer Levin. Most were there for Robert
Chambers. The girls who giggled. The boys who attended the
girls who giggled.

Raf would pick them off, like a sniper, take them to a corner
of the corridor, and talk about the case. Raf knew about Chambers' new girlfriend, Shawn Kovell. He wangled an interview
and it was depressingly sappy. Shawn was like her name, a
dopey young thing who said that Robert was a sweet boy who
could not hurt anyone and that people who knew him—really
knew him—could never believe all those horrible things they
were saying in the press.

One day, however, Raf came into Brennan's office and closed the door.

"I heard something," he said. "Kid I know from Dorrian's, he told me that there's a tape."

"What kind of tape?"

Raf shrugged. "A tape."

During the Christmas season, on the eve of the opening salvos of the actual trial, Chambers was said to have attended a party and done some dope with a bunch of the prep school girls. It had allegedly taken place on the same day as a motion had been made for cameras in the courtroom. The motion had been denied. If there was such a tape, Chambers had thumbed his nose one more time at the world.

"You gotta try to get it," Brennan said.

"If it exists. I heard it was destroyed."

"You gotta get it."

So Raf went to Litman and put his feet up on a table and asked about the interview that they both knew was never coming, and Litman did his usual matador evasion. Then Raf said he had heard about an incriminating videotape.

"We know that your guy made a tape and he's doing coke on it."

Litman stopped. "No," he said. "Maybe he's smoking a joint, but not coke."

Raf didn't say anything, he just nodded, but Litman had told him indirectly that a tape existed and that the rumors of it fluttering around the case were true. It was amazing. We were home video seekers, but this one sounded improbable, crazy. A tape of Chambers? I did not know about it, by the way. Raf was deep cover, on a mission. When he is possessed, Raf keeps it pretty close to the vest.

He went back to the trial and spoke to his source again, and the source said he knew of a copy. They had not all been destroyed. The thing was, the source said, whoever had it would probably want money.

No deal, said Raf. We don't buy news. But the chain of phone calls had begun. Code names and whispered messages and hints. Raf met the source, bought him a big dinner, told him that it was not inconceivable that money could be found to purchase a tape. He would regard it as buying material, the way you would buy a book. But the one thing that he could not do was to buy it sight unseen. The source had to ask his source. The existing copy of the tape was out of state, safely tucked away in a safe deposit box.

When he called back, the source said he would arrange for a showing of the tape that afternoon. Raf contained himself. He grabbed Dunleavy and explained the situation. He didn't want to watch it alone, just in case the deal turned sour. He'd have a witness. If worse came to worst, he could interview Dunleavy about what he had seen on the tape.

But the important thing was to get the tape. As he remembers it, Raf walked out of the office and the sun was bright and the people were smiling, and he was certain that he could get the tape if it existed. He had the confidence of a safecracker. Raf and Dunleavy walked to the apartment on the Upper East Side and were ushered into a room, and then the people who had the tape played it. Raf and Dunleavy agreed beforehand that they would remain skeptical. No matter how good it looked, they would find fault, just to hold the price down, if nothing else.

They sat in the living room and watched the tape come on the screen and it took all of their control to remain calm. It was beyond any expectation. The tape had been made at a Christmas season pajama party, and Robert Chambers was the only male, surrounded by four nubile girls. They were all over him, playing sexual games. And then, at one point during this hellishly damning tape, Robert Chambers took a doll in his big hands and turned to the camera and twisted the doll's head around and said in a playful voice, "Oops, I think I killed it." He wore a warped, Satanic smile on his face when he said it. And there was Shawn, the girlfriend, among the pretty girls.

"Well, the quality's not so good," said Dunleavy as he watched the tape roll.

"Not certain it would show up on the air," agreed Raf.

"And the sound's bad."

But when they left the apartment, they both leaped into the air and uttered silent screams—both of them, the same gesture, simultaneously. Nothing like it had ever been on the air before. It was incriminating in the most important way. You were looking at a soulless, cruel person in that tape. You were looking into the heart of darkness.

The empty-headed girls who surrounded him were a chilling chorus for an evil piper.

At the same time, the trial ended and the case went to the jury on St. Patrick's Day of 1988. When they stayed out too long and appeared deadlocked, Chambers agreed to plead guilty to first-degree manslaughter. He was pressed to admit at the sentencing that he intended to harm her. He would be eligible for parole in five years.

The public was unsatisfied. There was conflicting medical testimony, and when he made his sorry admission at the sentencing, Robert Chambers kept shaking his head in denial. Shawn Kovell clung to that during her interview with Raf. Did you see him shaking his head? she asked.

Raf knew that he needed the tape, to cement the case he had been building in his own mind. The trouble was that the people who owned the tape wanted $25,000 for it. Raf was not going to go that high. He offered $10,000. The negotiations went on, and it seemed as if a deal had been struck, but there was some understandable balkiness on the other side. Maybe someone told them what they were hawking.

On that final day, a Friday in May, Raf came into the office thinking that the deal was sealed and Dunleavy shook his head.

"They called it off, mate," he said.

Raf decided to copy a leaf from Robert Kennedy during the Cuban Missile Crisis. He called his source and told him that everything was set and he was ready to deliver the money. He was going with the earlier, friendlier message. The source agreed and the exchange of tape and the ten thousand dollars was made in an out-of-state bank, with no witnesses.

I was driving in New Jersey on that Sunday when I heard a radio bulletin that *A Current Affair* had obtained a damning tape of Robert Chambers cavorting on the eve of his trial and playing death games with a doll. When I got home, Connie said it was on the tube. I called Peter and he said something that he had said to me a hundred times: "Mate, you've got to trust me on this one."

When I got to work that Monday morning, Brennan rushed me into his office and closed the door.

"I had to do it this way, mate."

"Why? Why couldn't you let me in on it?"

"For two reasons. You're too clean and Dunleavy's too dirty. You'd open that honest mouth of yours and say, 'We paid money for the tape and I'm against it.'"

"You're right," I said, going to work.

I hosted the show and it was a blockbuster—the biggest

ratings ever at that time period. We showed it over and over, and we will continue to show it because it is a glimpse into something that we never see.

The rest of the press got very emotional about the tape, accused us of checkbook journalism—accused us of everything—but the family of Jennifer Levin came to our defense. They called a press conference and announced that they were glad that the tape had been shown. It was a fresh wind and it would blow away any doubts about the true nature of Robert Chambers.

We proved the value of home videotapes. Brennan, who understood these things, had given out the most important parts to the media on the Sunday before we broadcast this show. It didn't matter what they showed—we got the credit and the promotional hit, so the public was stunned into tuning in that night.

The Chambers story with the eerie videotape put *A Current Affair* on the country's dinner plate. Nationally, we were born.

Chapter Twelve

SIR James Carruthers was our chief ombudsman and rabbi. When Rupert said no, Sir James would clear his throat and take him aside and quietly convince him that he was making a mistake. And sometimes Rupert would change his mind. From Sir James, Rupert tolerated dissent. Sir James was one of those natural aristocrats who wore Savile Row suits and custom-made shirts and a regimental necktie.

He was a pixie of a man with royal bearing, but nonetheless descended from the usual outcasts and rogues who had settled Australia. Of course Sir James was a commercial bandit like the rest of Rupert's outlaw gang of scoundrels. He had spent most of his life as a publisher and editor in Australia, plundering the field of journalism with the best of them, but he had been given a knighthood for his contributions to the empire, as well as for his conspicuous success in business, even though he

was but a manager and Rupert had bought his owners out—
that is, he had bought his newspapers. The one other stipulation of the sale had been that Sir James would stay on as a
consultant, a senior vice president in charge of news. Rupert
sent Sir James all over the world to study his assets and to come
back and tell him candidly what he thought about his invest-
ments. He credited Sir James with superior insight and independent intelligence. He was never just another yes-man.

Rupert had wanted Sir James' papers, but he had wanted his
unimpeded wisdom as well, which he respected deeply. Even
more than that, he had wanted some of Sir James' style to rub
off on his works. Here was a man with a titled name and a
devilish mind that rivaled Brennan's.

Sir James was a consultant for the show, and he remained
an unbridled enthusiast and our direct link to the boss. If we
told Sir James at night, Rupert would know by morning. Sir
James calmed Rupert's nervous waters when we went after
Princess Di and Donald Trump and Malcolm Forbes.

Sir James understood from the first that we were a wayward
operation and had to be treated with underhanded privileges.
He knew what we were up to, and it was through his constant
intercession that Rupert kept his hands off. There were, however, moments when I felt the fingernails of Rupert's long
reach.

"He wants you to say something at the end of the broadcast," said Ian Rae one day, shortly after we began *A Current
Affair*.

"Really?"

"Something distinctive. Something that people will remember."

"How about if I tick like the *60 Minutes* clock?"

"He has something in mind."

"Like what?"

"He would like you to say, 'Good night, America.' "

"But there are stations which air the show in the afternoon. We'll sound stupid saying good night in the middle of the day."

"Nevertheless."

Brennan shrugged. Ian Rae shrugged. Sir James frowned. I read permission into that frown from Sir James, and when I got on the air, I invented a distinctive signoff which left me in the clear: "Until next time, America."

Sir James smiled and said, "Nicely done, Maurice."

Sir James always called me Maurice. He pronounced it "Morris." He was the only person in that entire cast of characters who called me by my correct name and pronounced it correctly. It was a small thing among all the other details, and I took it as a refined gesture of respect.

Once, Sir James and I were sitting at an Emmy Award ceremony as I watched the categories go by and the *Current Affair* nominations sink one by one from victory.

Sir James recognized my disappointment, slapped me on the back, and said, "Maurice, cheer up. We don't win awards. We win viewers."

As it turned out, Sir James had his work cut out for him. Something strange happened after the first splurge of success, when the markets opened up and started to come to us and the critics began to show some respect: Rupert got cold feet. Maybe it was that lingering thirst for respectability, maybe it was the cumulative insult of all of those upturned noses at the formal audiences of society—whatever it was, Rupert wanted to clean up *A Current Affair*.

We were across the street at The Racing Club and Sir James shook his head. The man wants to knock off Koppel again, he said. Rupert had always been obsessed by Ted Koppel—had even created *A Current Affair* to run against *Nightline* and show Americans how Australians did the news. Besides that, Rupert was accumulating points with the FCC. He would soon be in a fight with Teddy Kennedy over media monopoly rights in Boston, where he had acquired a TV station as well as a newspaper, and he wanted the taste police as allies. He wanted important and responsible interviews with world leaders and moguls, the kind that Barbara Walters got. The kind that put our audience to sleep.

"Don't worry about it, Maurice," said Sir James. "He'll see the error of his ways."

I hoped he was right.

While Sir James held off Rupert, we kept on rolling with our daily fix of silliness, irony, and tub-thumping anger. And in all that time, no one was sillier than Gordon Elliott. He was appalling. Gordon had not been a founding member of our crew. We'd been leaner then (in every sense of the word) and there'd been an abiding dread of too many Australians aboard. Gordon had had to fight his way into the shop. He had come to America after establishing himself as a celebrated and popular radio and television character in Australia, where he had worked as an anchorman, talk show host, gossip reporter, and, above all, world-class prankster. At the age of thirty-one he was globally famous for his improbably public antics. Just what we needed—another clown! And so, in the winter of 1987, Ian Rae and Brennan could no longer put him off—afraid, no doubt, of what he might do in retaliation—and they put him on the staff on the theory that it was safer than leaving him loose.

When he first walked into our office, with its wall of homage to Elvis and its James Dean posters and enemy dartboards, when he saw the clerical staff tossing footballs back and forth across the room, over the heads of writers bent into their keyboards like monks, when he sniffed the odor of disrespect for authority that permeated our every waking moment, he knew that he had arrived at his true spiritual destination.

As a tryout we sent him out to do the impossible.

At the time, Bill Cosby was at the height of his fame and at the furthest reach of his usual arm's length from the press. It was the Christmas season and Gordon knew that Cosby lived in an East Side town house and that he had refused to grant an interview. He said no to almost everyone. Cosby valued his privacy. To an ordinary reporter this might have constituted an answer to a request. To Gordon Elliott it posed a puzzle.

Christmas, he thought. What goes with Christmas? Carols. So Gordon Elliot decided to hire the New York Choral Society—all 110 voices belonging to 110 throats—to stand under the window of Bill Cosby's town house and serenade the TV star with Christmas carols. The trouble was that our show's budget did not provide for the customary $10,000 fee to pay the singers to stand under Cosby's window and sing. Gordon went to the leader of the choral society and negotiated. He said that he would give them $1,000 toward their expenses, and he would put them on television, and he promised them that they would get a chance to meet Bill Cosby.

It was probably the chance to meet Bill Cosby that sealed the bargain, plus the impish enthusiasm of Gordon Elliott, which was amazingly contagious and very hard to resist in the flesh.

Dressed in tails and holding music stands, the dignified

choral group assembled outside of Cosby's house at eight in the morning, cleared their throats, and broke into the Hallelujah Chorus from the *Messiah*. It must have thrilled more than one resident of that hushed neighborhood to awake on that crisp Christmas-season morning and hear such remarkable sounds.

The choral group switched to pop carols and sang "Silent Night," then went through the repertoire of every singer of carols and hymns, from Perry Como to Bing Crosby to Frank Sinatra to Handel. For two solid hours, they broke the frosty air with seasonal songs, with a camera crew going all the time, and cheerful, bouncing Gordon Elliott rousing the chorus whenever the energy flagged or hope dimmed. Between songs someone fetched coffee and donuts and somewhere along the way, the heart of Bill Cosby melted, because at ten o'clock he appeared at his door with that sheepish grin of his. And he gave Gordon Elliott his interview.

The man would not be denied. The people at Fox tried to tone him down on the theory that he was too exotic for the American taste, with his Liverpool/Australian iconoclasm. But you could not repress him. After all, he'd been at it since he was a kid. At twelve he had been over six feet tall and two hundred pounds and become, as a matter of self-defense, the class buffoon. By the time he was thirty-one, he was six foot seven and three hundred and thirty pounds, and he went wherever he wanted to go. He was a jolly giant man-child with an Irish wit as tangy as a nip in the air.

It was Gordon Elliott who stumped Trump. This was about a year later, in December of 1988, when Soviet President Mikhail Gorbachev was in New York on an informal visit. The leader had been invited to visit the lavish Trump Tower on Fifth Avenue, but schedules were running late and time was tight, and Gorbachev—who had met Trump at the White House during an earlier state dinner—canceled his visit. There had been some criticism about his stopover at a temple of material excess, but that was not the stated reason for canceling the tour. In any event it was a shattering disappointment for a man of Trump's skyscraper ego.

Kind soul that he was, Gordon decided to make Trump happy. On December 6, while Gorbachev was safely lunching with officials in New York, Gordon hired a stretch limousine, put a camera crew through the dome, and brought along some trailing cars from the news division to make it look like a real entourage. He hired a few knockout models—because Gordon was always thinking of flash and glamour and had absorbed Peter Brennan's rule that sex always pays off in a story—and planted them in the backseat of the limousine. Between them he put Ronald V. Knapp, an actor and rubber salesman who had won a Gorbachev lookalike contest. And off they went down Fifth Avenue at the lunch hour, causing some commotion and no little fuss.

They stopped at Tiffany's and at Saks, as Gorbachev surely would have done had he made this same tour, and then Ronald Knapp, with his artificial purple birthmark on his own dome, stepped out of the limo, waved to the crowd, smiled discreetly, and strolled along the avenue with his fake convoy of reporters and actors.

The shoppers and passersby were taken in. "Hey, Gorby!" they yelled, and Mister Knapp would wave and smile, and responded with what he thought was a Russian-accented "Hi!"

Meanwhile, Donald Trump had been alerted. Aides had rushed to his office high in the Tower and reported that the head of the Soviet Union was about to keep his historic rendez-

vous with the head of all of the Trump casinos and hotels.
Experts on such matters—public relations advisers—told Donald Trump that protocol probably demanded that he be out
front to receive Gorbachev, since, silly as it may have seemed
to people who kept track of property values and net worth, the
Russian President outranked Trump. Gorby's empire was
probably worth more if you included the Baltic states. This
was before the junk bond collapse of the Trump empire and
his own Taj Mahal defections.

Trump hurried down from his office, buttoned his suit
jacket, and fought his way through the wedge of phony security
people to our man, who was out on the street, smiling and
waving to the folks. "Good to see you again," Trump said with
that famous Trump smile. The "again" referred to the earlier
White House meeting, an official blur, but which Donald
Trump now believed in his heart had made him and Gorbachev
almost childhood pals.

Donald was actually blushing, caught up in the bigness of
the moment. Gordon Elliott stood back and allowed the event
to play itself out. Finally, because he was not a complete fool,
Donald noticed something odd: a television crew poking out of
the dome of the limousine. "Russian television," explained
Gordon helpfully. Then Donald saw the two women in the
back of the limousine and a kind of smoke alarm went off.
Something whispered to him that the head of all the Russias
would not travel openly around New York City with two very
conspicuous bimbos in the backseat. Not if he had a fiery wife
like Raisa. If Donald read women correctly, Raisa would have
buried him in the Kremlin Wall before permitting hanky-
panky, unless, of course, Raoul Felder had worked out an even
better and more airtight prenuptial agreement for Gorbachev
than he had for Donald Trump.

Still, Trump was a little reluctant to give in, to admit that he had been fooled. Besides, what if he was wrong and insulted a man who, in spite of his economic and political woes, still had a substantial nuclear arsenal? All he had was the *Trump Princess.*

Gordon took pity and turned to the camera and spoke loud enough for even Donald to hear: "I think he worked it out." Trump tried to smile, but he did not like being fooled. Gordon had taken the curse off the joke by giving Trump credit for working it out. In the end, he was kind and gave Trump a way out, which made such pranks possible.

Afterward, Trump issued formal statements denying that he had been fooled. His press people gracelessly called around town, telling the various gossip journalists, on the record, that he had known all along that it was not the real Gorbachev, but that he was such a good sport that he had gone along with the joke.

But if you watched the tape and saw the color leave his face with pale comprehension, you could see that he had been completely and utterly fooled.

Such a trick was not just silliness, mind you. In fact it was at the heart of our work, an attack on the pretentious, the pompous, and the mighty—a deeply committed *Front Page* style of sneaky irreverence. We used it again that year in a story that made quite a few headlines and gave comedy writers enough material to last them for months.

At the 1988 Democratic convention in Atlanta, Rob Lowe, the actor, there in support of his candidate, got into a ticklish situation with some underage fans. In fact, he videotaped what can only be described as pornographic tapes with a girl who worked in a beauty salon. It bore looking into. Our reporter on the case was Bill McGowan, who had come out of Fordham University and won a couple of Emmy Awards for writing and producing at CBS, and was now an original member of our unbridled police, first as a field producer, then as one of our best reporters. We sent him down to Atlanta in hot pursuit of the home videos, which we knew were being shown publicly in Atlanta nightclubs, mostly gay Atlanta nightclubs, because Rob Lowe, we heard, was rather, uh, handsomely endowed.

McGowan got down there and began a search for the tape, which was not too difficult since all of Atlanta was in on the secret. The problem was that another show was after the tape as well. Craig Rivera, the brother of Geraldo Rivera, was working as a producer and reporter for *Inside Edition,* a copycat show. Not willing to be beaten by Geraldo's brother, McGowan found out where the reporter was staying and made an anonymous call to his room, telling Craig to wait there, sit tight, that he would bring him a copy of the tape.

So Craig waited there all day while McGowan was free to chase the story, interview the girls, and return home with the video.

Rob Lowe went nuts, but he couldn't deny the facts. He attacked me on the air, but I didn't take offense—I offered him rebuttal time. Eventually the courts made him pay a substantial penalty to the family of the sixteen-year-old girl in Atlanta, and he received a sentence of twenty hours of community service. He went to a prison and spoke to hardened criminals about acting as a career.

Not long after that, I was at a Knicks game in Madison Square Garden when quite by accident I found myself sitting near none other than Rob Lowe. I was there with my daughter, Susan, who was unaware of the fuss our mutual presence was causing; however, the sportscaster, Marv Albert, got so excited he forgot the game and began to describe the encounter between Maury Povich and Rob Lowe.

"There's Povich getting up and approaching Lowe, he looks up and registers a moment of complete surprise! Lowe gulps and fumbles. What a move by Povich!"

I had one of those big smiles on my face. Rob Lowe looked a little sheepish. "You know, Maury," he said, "I did a few radio shows today."

He had gone on radio and tried to insult me, saying that people couldn't tell the difference between Dan Rather, a journalist, and Maury Povich, "an idiot." I knew all about his remarks. We'd used the excuse to show the tape again, or at least as much as we could get away with showing.

Lowe shook his head, which excited Marv Albert.

"He's shaking his head, ladies and gentlemen. Rob Lowe is shaking his head!"

I was big about it. "It's okay," I said.

"I really didn't mean it," said Lowe. "I don't mind you. It's your show I can't stand. You know, I love your wife."

He held out his hand.

"He's holding out his hand. Rob Lowe is shaking the hand of Maury Povich!"

My daughter Susan didn't even notice. She was entranced with Jon Bon Jovi, who was sitting just a few seats away.

That was not the end of the Rob Lowe affair. Audrey Lavin was our West Coast correspondent. A long-haired brunette, she had developed a seductive style for getting interviews. She would show up at the door of a star's home bearing flowers or bagels, depending on which she thought would work. Once, Peter Brennan had had a brilliant idea. He wanted an interview with Victoria Principal. There was nothing doing with

Victoria Principal, except for the fact that there were rumors of a lurid past and it would give us an excuse to delve into it and allow Peter to run a headline that he was dying to use: VICTORIA'S SECRET.

Audrey showed up at Victoria's door with her usual bouquet of flowers, and Victoria, who has almost no sense of humor, called Barry Diller, the head of Fox, to complain. Listen, we told Diller, that's Audrey. That's the way she works. She's the girl who sent a videotape of herself in Batman shoes and a Batman hat to Jack Nicholson, saying, in that squeaky little voice of hers, that she would do anything—"anything!"—for an interview. Jack had her over for dinner and she swam in his pool, but he did not give her an interview. We showed a little bit of that, and afterward, when the audience had heard that little-girl voice, I said on the air: "Audrey should stop sucking helium."

We sent our A-team—Audrey—after Lowe for one final interview. The trouble was in getting close. His house in Malibu was surrounded by the usual pack of reporters who tracked stories about sex and glamour and politics—so Audrey hired a Rob Lowe lookalike to draw them off. It worked for a moment . . . but she still didn't get inside for an interview.

As you can tell, we were not always successful, but we were always inventive and brave and nothing illustrated that better than another storm that hit America with gale-force winds. You see, what Rupert didn't understand was as far as *Nightline* was concerned, we had already beaten Koppel, and Rupert had never even noticed. The PTL scandal was ours, a televangelist Watergate, and we were the Woodward and Bernstein.

The Rev. Jim Bakker and his wife, Tammy, were the Ozzie

and Harriet of the PTL religious television network. It stood for Praise the Lord, although wags would later argue that it stood for Pass the Loot. Every week, Rev. Jim and Tammy would go on the air and make a tearful, passionate, and pious appeal for more money. The network was always on the verge of ruin. No matter how much they took in—and they took in plenty—it was never enough. The televangelist market was pumping out money like oil wells. It seemed as if a whole industry was out there throbbing, swallowing wholesale the savings and paychecks of ordinary citizens, orphans and widows, as well as little old ladies in tennis sneakers.

With all that money and all that temptation, it was just a matter of time until some of those deadly sins began showing up among the fundamentalists, who were, after all, human, and thus flawed with the usual quota of envy, lust, and greed. Besides, they were all after the same religious market. As a creature of television who had come to understand the business end, I could easily see how such a thing could happen.

Well, the inevitable happened. Rev. Jim Bakker was caught paying off a nice-looking church secretary named Jessica Hahn to keep silent about their moonlighting encounters. Her figure cost Jim Bakker six figures, which had reportedly come out of PTL funds.

It was a very touchy subject. It was religion! However, it was that hot, Southern, revivalist variety in which fiery evangelists whipped themselves into a fever trying to inspire a rebirth of faith and the parishioners got cleaned out paying the freight.

There were stories leaking out of the Southern newspapers and the church organs about the growing scandal. Investigations were launched. Boards of inquiry were commissioned. We covered it all, but we wanted the nub of the case. We wanted an interview with Jessica Hahn.

As I've mentioned, they had a few names for Dunleavy. "The Night Prowler" was one. "Street Dog" was another. They all gave a hint of tenacity, a whiff of his obstinacy. He reminded me of those villains in horror movies—you think you've killed them and they rise up from the dead, dripping blood, shot four times and cut in half, but still coming at you. That was Dunleavy. There was no way to stop him from coming at you.

He was the man we sent after Jessica Hahn.

In late April of 1987, since there was no pressing national crisis, there was no bigger story than the Jim and Tammy Bakker scandal. It had everything: Jim Bakker's sexual liaison, financial misconduct, and the strange behavior of his wife, Tammy, a religious singer who had reportedly had her own dalliance with a country singer. She also had the spending habits of a Saudi princess. The lavish homes and expensive wardrobe did not seem to bother the public as much as the air-conditioned dog house. That, and the way she looked. She was an amply endowed woman, and she might even have been attractive, but we'd never know because she insisted on wearing clown makeup. She had eye makeup that overflowed and spilled down her face with the regularity of a riverbank at flood. The woman could not stop weeping, and bravely smiling, all at the same time, with the mascara and tears cutting ridges in the pancake on her cheeks.

Once she wept for more donations for her church as well as for that air-conditioned doghouse. Now she wept for poor Jim and Tammy and the cruel way that the government and the other fundamentalists—waiting in the wings to take over their lucrative televangelist network—had come down upon them, without any Christian charity or love. Over and over, she and brave Jimmy appealed for support. They had taken refuge in their multimillion-dollar sanctuary in Palm Springs, California. From time to time they would emerge and deny everything to the semicircle of reporters and camera people.

After our first reports, the story moved from the back pages of the *New York Times* steadily forward, as rumors began about financial troubles.

The story now was Jessica Hahn. She was meant for us.

Dunleavy had staked out the outside of Jessica's apartment in Massapequa, Long Island, trying for an interview. We had done an entire show from the PTL park in South Carolina and we felt a certain proprietary interest in getting her first and putting her version of the events on the air. Dunleavy tried everything. He pleaded. He begged. He promised her fame and fortune in their long, late-night telephone conversations. But she wouldn't budge.

He came back and told this to Peter Brennan as they sat across the street at The Racing Club, swilling beer after beer, sucking cigarettes, shaking their heads at her stubborn holdout. Finally Peter had an inspiration.

"Where is she?" asked Brennan.

"Rented a couple of rooms on the second floor of a house out on Long Island," replied Dunleavy.

"Well, there you go, love."

"Where?"

"To the Island. We'll sing her down."

And so the two drunken Australians climbed into the backseat of a cab and drove out to Long Island, where they surrounded themselves with six-packs of beer, planted themselves on the curb outside of Jessica Hahn's window, and proceeded to serenade her with a range of ballads, from "I'll Take You Home Again, Kathleen," to "Danny Boy." The empty cans of the dwindling six-packs came in handy to keep time.

They did not get a response—not from Jessica, at any rate. But they did get a reaction from the Suffolk County Police. The cops did not arrest Dunleavy, whom they had come to know and love in the way all police did, but they did issue some stern advice about singing loud songs at four o'clock in the morning on a suburban sidewalk. It violated some municipal code and made the neighbors nervous. Worst of all, it didn't work.

Finally, everything broke apart. I was at my desk on Monday, April 27, 1987, watching the news, when I was struck in the face with a ten-second promo for *Nightline*. It was Ted Koppel. "Tonight," he said, "our guest will be Jessica Hahn, in her first interview since the scandal broke."

I ran across the street to The Racing Club.

"Where's Dunleavy?" I screamed, barging through the door.

Ian Rae looked over and replied: "I sent him out on another story, mate."

There had been an attempted hit on John Gotti, the Mafia's glamorous "Dapper Don," who had clawed his way to the top of New York's Gambino crime family. Rae had pulled Dunleavy off of Jessica and sent him out to Queens to cover the Gotti story.

"He's the only one who can get the story," said Rae. "For the nightly news."

This was probably true, but all things being equal, we needed Dunleavy more than the news needed him. I appealed to Rae in a way that he would understand, him being so slavish to Rupert's obsessions. "Ian, Ted Koppel just announced that he's got her for *Nightline.*"

Ian dropped his bottle of beer on the floor and ran to the phone. He got Dunleavy, who had just spent an hour and a half fighting his way through traffic to get into town; he'd shot his footage around the Gotti hangout, given the tapes to a Channel 5 reporter, and, on his own, was back on the road, heading for Islip. Which is where Ian Rae caught up with him. Back on Long Island, he talked his way into the house, past the owner, who had taken pity on Dunleavy, having grown fond of him after all those weeks of camping on her doorstep.

"Goddamn it! How can you do this to me?" screamed Dunleavy. He was yelling through two doors, where Jessica had barricaded herself. "You really want to go on *Nightline* instead of *A Current Affair*? Jessica, how can you do this to me?"

Jessica was on the phone to her adviser in Portland, Oregon. This was the man who had arranged her $260,000 scholarship from the PTL. He could hear Dunleavy through both doors and three-thousand-odd miles away. Dunleavy heard Jessica talking into the phone, telling her adviser that she felt sick.

Just then a long limousine pulled up and the driver started heading for the house. Dunleavy assumed an air of supreme authority.

"Who are you?"

"I'm here to pick up Jessica Hahn. I have to take her to New York. She's on *Nightline* tonight."

Dunleavy shook his head. "She can't go. She's sick. She may have to go to the hospital."

The driver turned around and headed back to the Apple. Dunleavy headed back to his perch, up against her bedroom door. "Jessica, I'm sorry you're sick. You can't go on *Nightline*. You have to go to the hospital and find out if it's serious."

The woman who owned the house nodded gravely. "Maybe that is the best thing to do," she said.

Dunleavy ordered an ambulance. Five minutes later Jessica

emerged, her arms folded across her stomach, and got into the ambulance with her landlady and Dunleavy.

I knew none of this. I was at home with Connie, and my palms were sweaty as I heard the *Nightline* theme come up. Koppel came on the screen. "First, a schedule change. Earlier this evening, Jessica Hahn, who was going to join us later in the program, went briefly to a hospital. She was seen by a doctor, treated, and is now back home. I spoke to her a short time ago and she'll be joining us at another time."

He did it. The amazing Dunleavy had given Ted Koppel a bellyache. I leaped out of the bed, my fist raised in the air, and howled.

Connie was a little more sober.

"Maury," she explained. "It's *A Current Affair.*"

A few days later Dunleavy did indeed get his exclusive interview with Jessica Hahn. There she was, in her chaste white suit and long silver earrings, her hands folded like a good girl, confessing her sins to our chief newshound. "Nothing good came out of that" encounter with Jim Bakker, she said, except that the fundamentalist sects were all fighting. Jerry Falwell was trying to take over the PTL Network, and Tammy Faye was saying that she wanted to shoot herself, and our Dunleavy asked a question that sounded sappy.

"Could you ever fall in love?"

Jessica sat there, her eyelids suffering under the weight of Tammy Faye's eye makeup influence, her bee-stung lips rouged thick, and stammered for long seconds. Then she said, "God can heal anything."

The networks would follow us and she would reveal what she had to reveal, then, after a series of cosmetic operations, vanish into a kind of third-rate media obscurity, making guest appearances on talk shows until the public tired of her.

But all that attention under her window paid off. We had her first. The Night Prowler had struck again.

Chapter
Thirteen

WE were all over the place, hitting every slick magazine cover, winning every market. It was a fine, high season when we knocked off the game shows and edged out the reruns and stomped the dry, arid normal news programs with our campy and light-fingered approach to the world's events. We had become a force.

There were articles written about our success—deep thinkers who probed and took us apart and examined, in a very cautious way, the unexpected appeal that we had to the American public. I could tell by the type of coverage we were getting that we had moved into some strange new category of programming for which they had no word and no description.

Newsweek ran a cover story on "shock" television, and I felt protected, because my own beloved sister, Lynn, was a senior editor at the magazine. The only thing that I asked the reporter was that I not be paired with Morton Downey Jr., because we were definitely not in the same league and should not be cast in the same category. Downey was mean-spirited and self-righteous, and we were high-spirited and self-deprecating. What could be more different?

Sure enough, what did *Newsweek* do? They paired me up with Morton Downey, and called it "The Odd Couple of Sensationalism," and when I objected and asked my own beloved sister how they could do such a thing to her own beloved brother, she shrugged and said she agreed with the comparison. "I think it's fair," she said.

She still didn't get it. Nobody in my family got it except maybe my father. But never mind—I was having the time of my life, and I have to admit I did have some hand in my image as a perceived media desperado. I would say things off the top of my head on the air, such as, "Some shows go to the edge . . . we take it one step further: we are the abyss." I made fun of us, shaking my head and scowling at the stories of bikini-clad coeds running wild at spring break, or show some justified ambivalence when we did a story about Brigitte Nielsen, whose breasts popped out of her strapless leather gown on the dance floor. I scared the hell out of the Fox executives and lawyers with my unconcealed opinion about my own show.

To me, the size of the show's success was inconceivable. I had grown accustomed to spending my life in a frantic effort to keep my head above water. Staying alive seemed a reasonable goal, and now, suddenly, I was a host with a growing list of stations fighting for the rights to our show. I reminded myself that I was an overage, overnight star who would soon turn fifty, but I had never tasted that rare wine of national recognition and it was heady.

There was also big money at stake. I had no idea of the scope because I remained a wide-eyed idealist who thought I was still selling war bonds. Annuities and stock options and zero coupon bonds sounded to me like comic-book characters. It did not occur to me that I was a valuable commodity who had raised the advertising cost-per-minute with my nightly displays of tolerant permission and dignified scorn. Nevertheless, my new status was driven home one day when David Nuell, who ran Paramount's *Entertainment Tonight,* called and began a friendly conversation.

"What a great show," he said. "Just great. Look, we're thinking about doing a segment about it on *E.T.* Maury, would you send me the logs of your stories? You know, for the segment."

I laughed. We were in deadly, head-to-head competition in all markets and they were about to launch a segment of the show called "Inside Story," and he wanted me to give him the secret formula for our success.

As politely and as gently as I could manage, I refused, letting David know that I knew what he was up to. Within a month they started their segment, trying to get the flavor of *A Current Affair* into the "Inside Story" segment, but it didn't work. For one thing they could allow only two or three minutes to a story, while we could devote an entire show. For another, they were slick and packaged and it looked like fiction, while we were rough-cut. And they did not have our flair: they did not have Brennan or Dunleavy. Later, Paramount would copy us entirely with its show *Hard Copy.*

It was about the same time, a year into the show, that I began to see our stories cropping up on network newscasts. Jim and Tammy Faye Bakker would never have been part of the traditional news programs if we had not cracked it wide open. From page 39 of the *New York Times* to page one.

Another time came when we hit upon the story of Sid Bass, the megamogul from Forth Worth, Texas, who owned twenty-five percent of Disney's stock, among all of his other holdings. The oldest of four sons of one of the wealthiest families in America, he was a genuine third-generation billionaire whose assets ran from oil to Fairchild Industries to publishing: a takeover shark. His great-uncle was the wildcat speculator Sid Richardson, who'd been an adviser and buddy of Lyndon Johnson. Like a lot of blooded royalty, the Bass clan shunned vulgar publicity, and in that enclave of 400,000 citizens of Forth Worth, thirty miles west of Dallas, their writ ran strong. They guarded their privacy with the same imperial caution with which they ran their investment empire. No one spoke of their private lives for fear of inviting the Bass wrath. The family had clearly grown reticent since Uncle Sid, "the billionaire bachelor," had spelled out his philosophy on women: "[They're] all wantin' a landing field, but mine's fogged in."

His nephew Sid's landing lights were on. Married to Anne H. Bass, a blueblood who'd majored in Italian literature at Vassar, he'd nevertheless experienced that old familiar midlife itch. He was a man in his mid-forties who looked like the guy who rejects your application for a driver's license: a nondescript bureaucrat. We were as surprised as anyone when word began filtering out—although not in any highly public way—that he was about to toss over his wife, Anne, for a splashy New York socialite named Mercedes Kellogg.

It was, in the thin, sanitized air of that Southwest circle of wealth, nothing less than a civic meltdown. The upper crust of the entire jet set buzzed with the fact that he was seen with the glamorous Ms. Kellogg in, of all places, Mortimer's, a very trendy and very conspicuous New York eatery. Bass was a private guy who was not accustomed to the irreverence of the

New York media. He owned a big share of Texas and was accustomed to being addressed with hushed respect and obedient awe. No one dared arouse his ire.

We were made of sterner stuff. As soon as we heard about the rocky marriage and the new love interest, we sent Bill McGowan down to Fort Worth to blow it all open. Brennan began working on hot promotional copy. After a few days McGowan called in and said he had run into a stone wall. Sid Bass had a lock on everyone. Even the gossip columnist from the *Fort Worth Star-Telegram* came to an interview with her lawyer.

"I'm telling you, all I got is one still photograph and some very scared interviews," said McGowan in the conference call with me on one end and Brennan on the other. "This is gonna take time. Maybe we should come back later. Peter, I just have nothing."

"Mate," said Brennan, "I've got some good and some bad news; which do you want first?"

"Let's hear the bad news," said McGowan.

"Well, I've been running print ads all over the lot and the piece is gonna run tomorrow. Sorry, mate."

"What's the good news?"

"I lied. There is no good news."

Somehow McGowan came up with a piece. He went out and got man-on-the-street interviews. He got long-distance shots. He got file footage. He ran it like *Dallas,* calling it *Fort Worth,* with Sid Bass as old Ewing, and it seethed with a lot of understated passion. It was a great piece, but it didn't say one single thing that hadn't already been said.

The next day, when I introduced it, I was embarrassed by the story's thinness, so I said, "I'm sure there's going to be a lot more to this story and we'll have it for you."

Well, the reaction to the story was hard to believe. Liz

Smith, whose syndicated column ran in over one hundred newspapers, said that *A Current Affair* was the best new investigative show on the air, and that we had broken the Texas juggernaut to lay bare the Sid Bass story. I sent her flowers.

A few weeks later I was down in Washington and I ran into Barry Diller, the chairman of the board of Fox, who said, "What do you mean, you're going to run another piece on Sid Bass?"

I'd forgotten that Diller was friends with Michael Eisner, the head of Disney, and that he was cheek-to-jowl with Sid Bass.

"I don't think we should have another Sid Bass story."

I didn't agree and we ran a few. We noted the fact that Sid Bass—that tight-lipped and thrifty legend—went out buying diamonds as big as the Ritz for his new sweetie. That spring, at Swifty Lazar's annual Oscar party in Hollywood, I was sitting there, minding my own business, when I felt a hand on my shoulder. It was Michael Eisner. "I want you to meet a friend of mine," he said, pushing Sid Bass into my face.

"Sid," I said, "before you say anything, let me introduce you to a good side of me," indicating Connie.

We all laughed.

Sid finally divorced Anne to marry Mercedes Kellogg. It cost him five hundred million dollars. We ran a piece about it.

Standard television practices demand that the reporters have a slightly detached view of themselves. However, passion and persistence are also valid techniques. You can tell a story from a closer, sharper perspective. That's how we also made our presence felt on network news. In 1988 I was interviewed for a *CBS Evening News* segment on the impact of tabloid television. I won't say that they were smug, but there was a certain patronizing tone to their report. They were amused by our little program.

On that same program, Rita Braver did a story about a child-custody case that was about to come before the Supreme Court. The father of seven-year-old Katey wanted to win custody from the stepparents. David Lee Miller had the only video of the child, which had been shot in a schoolyard. Rita Braver used the *Current Affair* tape, crediting us. It made for a nice ironic twist to the first story.

And then there was Ted Koppel. It wasn't enough that we had beaten him out of Jessica Hahn. In August 1989 we pointed out in our spoofing manner that the infallible Koppel had lifted satellite footage of our story of Malcolm Forbes' 70th birthday party in Morocco without permission. The make-believe staffers were make-believe "shocked." We had a phony grade school teacher, who said Koppel was jealous of me, and a phony dean of a journalism school, who said our rivalry went far back, and was not surprising since Koppel had once tried to change his name to "Ted Povich." It was straight out of *Take the Money and Run,* and it was funny.

We also hammered the point home by showing that Koppel's network, ABC, had borrowed our re-enactment technique with their story on Felix Bloch, the diplomat accused of passing along secrets to the Russians. Only they called it a "dramatization" and didn't let the public know where it began or ended. Peter Jennings ended up apologizing on the air. The problem wasn't that they had done it—it was that they hadn't done it *right.*

* * *

In the late summer of 1988 we were piling up syndication markets and I got a call from Roger King. It was a call from syndication's God. King was the biggest man in the syndication business, with the top three shows in the country, *Oprah, Wheel of Fortune,* and *Jeopardy:* a huge force in the industry. He was also, personally, an intimidating character, very large. The family fortune sprang from his father's peddling of the old-time children's classic *The Little Rascals.* We had already annoyed Roger when we had done a story about his getting involved in a legal fracas in Florida. Bill McGowan hadn't been able to do it straight because we'd have been accused of doing a witch-hunt on a competitor, so he'd done it like a game of *Jeopardy.* He'd gone to the beach, provided the answers, and had people ask the questions. It was hilarious, and our West Coast Fox machines had had to work day and night to duplicate the tape for all the people who wanted a copy. Every time Roger King saw me after that, he said, "You know, I could have sued you." He tried to sound good-natured about it, but it always made me a little uneasy, as if he'd really weighed that possibility, and even though he'd come down on the other side it lay there like a grudge.

However, in 1988 we were a hit, and he called and said he'd like to talk. I did not know what to make of it, being the *naif* that I am about such matters. Bob Young, one of the executive producers, came into my office and said, "We should have dinner, you, me and Brennan."

Young was a Welshman who'd worked for the *Star,* an old Murdoch guy with tabloid blood. He was in his mid-forties and was a child of instinct and sensation. I'd known him from the *New York Post* when he'd been the photo editor, sending people out to steal pictures and photographers to chase celebrities and stories. He knew every newshound and public relations agent in the world. He had the best contacts and the best sources because he understood that above everything, on a tabloid, you've got to have sources to get the picture.

He worked with Brennan and Dunleavy and Ian Rae, and he had a penchant for practical jokes. He kept sending pig pictures to Ian, because we all called Ian "the pig." There was another part of Young too. He could smell an opportunity. Bob had also been approached by the King people.

He wanted to feel us out. Brennan didn't disagree. It wasn't disloyalty to Rupert or anything underhanded. Brennan was too rich a personality for that kind of game. He overflowed with generosity. It was a matter of survival. He sensed a looming threat. He had gone to bat for me once too often. He had told Murdoch once too often that I was important to the show's success, and Murdoch did not want a star hosting the show. Murdoch wanted the stories to drive the show. He didn't want to be held prisoner to "talent." And when Brennan put his foot down and insisted that there could be no show without me, it counted against him and he knew it.

And so, in that deep part of his intellect where he told himself the truth, without sentimentality, Brennan knew that he had to provide for that day when Rupert would turn a cold eye to an old friend and let Brennan go. He said that we should have dinner and talk about Roger's feelings.

"Roger King is smart," he said. "He'll offer us ownership."

It was a good argument to someone who had always been an employee on sufferance.

There was one more guest at the dinner party we were getting ready to attend: John Tomlin. Tomlin was a young guy, mid-thirties, an American, *A Current Affair* original, and the only person apart from me who was a child of television. He'd produced *PM Magazine* and *Two on the Town,* and had started his own production company. All of the video equipment, including the shooters, were leased from Tomlin, who appreciated the value of ownership when it came to television. He wasn't very creative, not in the same way that Brennan was, but he was solid. He could stop last-minute panic and find a way to get something done. Technically, he understood that "this could be done," or something else couldn't.

He'd hired himself on as supervising producer, which we desperately needed, because nobody else knew how to edit or how to get something on the air. John was that guy. Brennan came up with the farfetched notions and John found a path to get it on the air. And he understood the spirit of the show and he marveled at it the way I did because, children of television that we were, we had never seen this sort of thing. The combination was amazing—these Australians unencumbered by rules and traditions, and American know-how! Tomlin was excited by it. He and Young seemed ready to jump.

The dinner was at a steak house on the West Side, and Bob and John started pressing Brennan and me. I was still a little leery. A few weeks earlier I'd seen Roger at a broadcasters' convention in Saratoga. Larry King was supposed to have interviewed Roger King. They'd wanted to call it "King on King." But at the last minute Larry had had to back out and he'd asked me to handle the interview. When they'd called Roger, he'd let out a yelp, saying that he should be suing me for that story we'd run about him in Florida. He relented though, and when we met at a cocktail party he looked at me and said again, "You know, I should be suing you." I said, "Oh, Roger, you don't want to do that. It was all in the spirit of fun."

Bob Young was very excited. He saw the dollar signs ahead. His eyes were like saucers. I had been bumped up to a nice salary and I thought that Fox would take care of me in the next round of negotiations, but it wasn't that that stopped me from thinking too hard or too long about Roger King's offer. It was that old notion of loyalty. Fox had made me the star I had become, and it would be ungrateful to abandon ship for something as crass as money. We'd only been syndicated for a year and we had one hundred stations and I thought, "We'll kill anybody else who comes along."

I just wanted to hear someone tell me how much they wanted me.

Bob Young heard the cash register. He saw the ownership. King will double and triple salaries and—here's the big clincher—he'll offer us points. I had heard that word before, but only in gambling halls when guys were shooting craps, or whispered among investors. I never thought that it applied to me.

Tomlin was also excited because he knew the people at King World and they were dangerous when they plunged. It was also a way to get Ian off of our backs.

Peter Brennan and I walked a little in the late summer night, clearing our heads from the steaks and wine. It was a bleak neighborhood and the people who came to dine had their limousines outside with the motors running. We didn't speak much, but then we never had to speak a lot. He knew what I was thinking and I knew what he was thinking.

Then he turned to me and smiled and said, "Not yet, mate. Not yet."

Chapter
Fourteen

*T*wo weeks later Bob Young and John Tomlin quit and
went to King World to put together *Inside Edition*.
There was a rumble under the earth. Suddenly Rupert realized
that he had no one under contract. Most of the talent working
at *A Current Affair* were on salary and were not contractually
bound to remain with the show. He had failed to protect
himself. It was not like Rupert.

And so, like all moguls and oligarchs who sense rebellion,
grumbling, and dissatisfaction in the ranks, Fox was angry, and
worried. Any packager with deep pockets could raid the staff
and eat up their syndicate. Barry Diller, the head of Fox
Television, was pissed. Rupert was pissed. Ian was pissed.
They started doubling and tripling salaries, and even then we
lost a couple of field producers and a desk editor. We even lost
Steve McPartlin, who was a solid reporter.

McPartlin looked like Clark Kent and had a wicked sense of humor. He assembled one of the great spoofs of our time: the great Peter Holm Telethon.

Peter Holm, the groom of actress Joan Collins, looked like someone bred in California. Blond, a little flaccid, no socks, and slow to catch on. He was handsome, in a dissipated sort of way, and he was younger than Joan Collins, but even that wasn't enough to keep them together. After a while she sued for a divorce. Peter, who had no real income, countersued for $80,000-a-month support, claiming that he was responsible for Joan's financial success in some mysterious fashion and, as proof, she had accumulated a substantial part of her wealth while they were together, and besides, he was entitled. For a while he camped out in her home and had to be run off by the sheriff. Our kind of guy.

In two short hours at the Fox studios in New York, Steve set up a phony phone bank with volunteers and balloons and a lot of noise. He rented a tuxedo and he made tearful pleas on Peter's behalf. He even undid his bow tie, like Jerry Lewis, a sure sign of the overworked and overwhelmed host of a genuine telethon for a very tragic cause: Save Peter Holm. He ran a scrawl of phony donations underneath. Mrs. Johnny Carson. Imelda Marcos. Connie Chung. We did breakaways with people offering to donate a flophouse bed and some deposit bottles, and then we'd cut back to Peter Holm himself, standing outside the courthouse in Los Angeles in his shiny silk suit with a grin cemented on his face, because he really didn't get it: he thought that we were running a real telethon for him. They ran a crawl with the phony telephone number—1-555-CALL HOLM.

We "raised" maybe $20, which appeared larger on McPartlin's "Peter Meter." McPartlin never let on that it was a gag.

And Peter Holm never caught on. At the end of the show, after we were off the air, he asked me how much we had raised.

On the First Anniversary tape of our show, McPartlin sat in as the host, and he had my daughter Susan, the lawyer, hold up a paper saying that she was going to sue me for $80,000 a month in supplementary income, seeing as how I'd come into my own and maybe I'd better get my brother, David, the hotshot lawyer, to defend me. McPartlin also showed old pictures of me, going way back when I was a kid in the sixties wearing wide-lapeled suits and a Beatles haircut. He had a great sense of humor; it had bite and substance, and he had a likable presence on the air.

We lost McPartlin. We lost Young and Tomlin, and King made it a war—which anyone who knew him could have predicted. His first press release announced that he had taken two of the creators of *A Current Affair*. Now we were left uncreated!

Still, he had a point. We knew that we were going to have big problems because they had people over there now who knew how it worked, understood what we were about. Then it was announced that David Frost was going to be the host, because King was not like Diller and Murdoch—he knew that he needed a signature on that show, someone that the public would recognize and take into their homes.

It was a bigger name than mine, much bigger, but Brennan and I talked it over and decided that they were making an important and basic mistake—namely, bringing in a foreign accent. From the first, Brennan and his people understood that you could not sell a foreign accent to an American audience. That was why they had brought me on the show in the first place. The Australians couldn't do it.

We sat at a table across the street, piling up empty beer

bottles, talking ourselves into believing that Roger King, the greatest syndicator in all of television, didn't know what the hell he was doing. It took quite a few beers.

"Well, mate," said Brennan, "David Frost is a well-known name, but he is not going to be able to put over a show like that."

"No, never," I replied, holding up my hand for a refill because I didn't want to lose this liquid courage.

What scared us more than David Frost was the fact that they were going into a very powerful New York outlet, Channel 4, the NBC flagship station, dead against us. I thought: Good God! Even if they were just a little bit successful, they were going to steal some of our ratings points. They would do that even if they were a failure. We were going to lose something no matter how *Inside Edition* turned out.

The crusher was when we learned that Roger King had budgeted $4 million just for promotion for the first eight weeks of the show. That set off a mild panic. Suddenly he had every spare moment of radio time in his pocket. We couldn't counterattack. There was no radio time available. They were running back-to-back promos. They had a few of our guys, they had the deepest pockets in television; they didn't even need a good show.

The Australians did what they always did when they got into trouble: they threw a party. They rented out the second floor of "21" and toasted our success and hired an unknown piano player named Harry Connick Jr., who would later go on to considerable fame himself. Meanwhile, though, Rupert began to hold meetings. The building held its breath as he came scowling through the halls and closed the door with Ian Rae and Peter Brennan. He brought in Gerald Stone to work as an executive producer. Rupert was impressed because Stone had been an executive producer of the Australian version of

60 Minutes. Stone was a very classy guy who had been born in America but had absorbed an Australian tactical killer instinct.

At the same time Rupert was starting another program—one with higher journalistic credentials, or at least pretensions—called *The Reporters.* A lot of people were being stripped from our staff. The most important, perhaps, were Dunleavy and Rafael Abramovitz. They were leaving to work on *The Reporters.* Between *Inside Edition* and *The Reporters,* we were getting very thin. Most of Rupert's attention had been devoted to that project until this thing with Roger King had exploded.

The Reporters was a doomed attempt to make a high-toned version of *A Current Affair,* and they did some good stories. Dunleavy interviewed killer drug lords and almost lost his life a dozen times. He spent more time in Colombia than he did in his home on Long Island. But it didn't work. They didn't have a host, and you could not convince those rock-headed people at Fox that someone was required to hold the show together. *The Reporters* lasted from fall of 1988 until the winter of 1990.

In late '88, however, Rupert felt Roger King breathing down his neck. When Brennan came out of the meeting with Rupert, after we'd first gotten wind of *Inside Edition,* we went across the street and I asked him, "So what happened?"

He needed a few beers to get lubricated.

"The most amazing meeting, mate. Rupert wants to know what it's going to take to combat this big, new, fucking competition. And all the Fox promotion people are there with their fucking yellow legal pads and they've got it fucking figured out on paper. It's gonna cost two million dollars. Minimum. 'Fine,' says Rupert. 'Do it.' The Fox guys all get shifty and nervous and say, 'Well, we have a problem.'

" 'What's the problem?' asks Rupert."

" 'The problem is that we don't have a way to dispense the money. There's no promotion department for *A Current Affair.*' We have no way to spend the two million dollars that Rupert is ready to take out of his pocket."

In any other company that decision would take months. Rupert said, "Do it, whatever it takes," because now it was a battle and he couldn't resist a good fight. This guy King had come in, thrown a lot of money around and bought his people, and somewhere down deep, Rupert knew that King had underestimated him. That's how Australians are, in the end: they take it all personally.

The people at Fox went out and did it. They found ways to spend Rupert's $2 million.

We had to hire a promotion department: five people. Before, we had promoted our own show on the air, and nationwide, Fox had spent a total of half a million dollars, which we had parceled out like pennies. With Rupert in a fight, however, we bought lots of radio time, and we gave away beer mugs and underwear and T-shirts and sweat pants.

Then Roger King made a few more crucial mistakes. The biggest was "attitude." He wanted to keep his skirts clean. Roger-the-truck-driver wanted to put a show on the air that would bring honor and credit to his name. This is a man who—when you come to his summer birthday party at his place on the New Jersey Shore, with all the media moguls there from every network, every studio, every television station group, where there are clowns and tables bending under the weight of gourmet food, and fireworks by the Grucci brothers that dwarf the Fourth of July show in New York City harbor—the first words out of his mouth are, "You're looking at a man who makes nine million dollars a week."

"With or without overtime?" I asked, and he looked perplexed.

To this day, Roger is the best salesman alive. He travels all over, selling pieces and chunks of shows and reruns, always selling himself. But, like a lot of people who acquire a great fortune, he began to think about his image. He wanted a polished version of *A Current Affair* under his name.

It was the start of 1989, and my agent, Alfred Geller, urged me to renegotiate my contract with Fox, as promised, because, he said, I would never be in a better position to bargain. Gerald Stone asked for five months, a grace period, so that it would bring them to late spring of 1989. It would also test whether or not *Inside Edition* would beat us out.

Geller was furious with me. "If you fail, you'll never get the money," he said. "This is the moment. The pot of gold. You've got a chance for catching lightning in a jar . . . they played to your weakness!"

He was right—but Fox had correctly looked me in the eye and tested my macho confidence. If I was so cocksure of myself, why wouldn't I give them the five months? Why wouldn't I beat out *Inside Edition?*

I agreed. I gave them the five months. Part of it was loyalty, but part of the reason was something else. It was the thrill of the competition. I had Brennan and I had great energy and I thought that we could beat them—even without Dunleavy, Young, Tomlin, Abramovitz, and McPartlin.

We went out and hired bodies. We had been decimated and now we were given a license to recruit and we got fat. More stations signed on. "Reality programming" was getting big and we were the daddy of reality programming.

The launch date for *Inside Edition* was January of 1989, and we went shopping around the satellites, trying to find out what stories they were going to do. That's how shows worked—they fiddled around with frequencies and latched onto the communications channels and listened in on the shop talk. It was spying. We all did it, switching around the dials, trying to pick up their satellite, pointing the transponders to find their bird so we could listen to their teleconferences and their stations, trying to winkle out their promotion campaign to find out what stories they were after.

They were also doing the same thing to us, because they knew how we worked and it was part of the game. Young and Tomlin were not there for nothing. I knew *Inside Edition* was into our computer because that's the way it is. Maybe it's illegal, but that's the *Front Page* mentality. So we changed codes and shifted tactics and locked them out of our computer. We did something else, too. We acted like soldiers sworn to secrecy about the invasion plans for D-Day. No one broke the silence.

Just before the New Year's launch, they made one more critical error. They let us find out their story. It sounded familiar.

Earlier that summer we'd done a story about a black prisoner in Florida named James Richardson who had been wrongfully accused of murdering his seven children twenty years before, in the late sixties. Mark Lane, the Kennedy-conspiracy lawyer and activist, had been shopping this story around and we'd been on it. There was no evidence against Richardson and he'd been in jail for a long time. The story ran, there was a lot of reaction, and the man finally got out of prison.

The week before the Monday launch date, we discovered that *Inside Edition* planned to do the Richardson story as their main lead. Somebody said to Brennan, "Hey, you know they're doing the James Richardson story."

And he said, in that Cheshire way of his, "Oh, really? Terrific!" And then he sent our reporter, Bob Martin, who'd done the first story and had a history with the man, back to

Florida. Martin secretly wrapped up another story with James Richardson. We swore Richardson and Mark Lane to secrecy and the whole thing was kept in-house. And on that Friday before the launch date, we ran the Richardson story again, with fresh updates and interviews.

Inside Edition was committed. They had spent all that money promoting their show and they couldn't change gears. They couldn't rip open the show over the weekend, and the day after their launch our publicists were calling around and saying, "Oh, well, you know that we did that story Friday." When the reviews came in on *Inside Edition,* despite what you thought of Frost or the show, the reviewers all pointed out that the lead story was one that had been done earlier on *A Current Affair.*

As it was, when *Inside Edition* opened in January of 1989, I thought that David Frost could have been a tad more graceful in his opening remarks. He said that they were going to be clean and pure and true blue. They were not going to do stories about three-headed babies (although I'd like to see anyone pass up that story), or use cheap gimmicks or sensationalize the news, like-some-other-shows-he-could-name.

I personally thought that he meant us.

Unlike those other nameless tacky shows, *Inside Edition* was going to be amazingly faithful to the pristine tenets of the best journalistic standards. They would, he swore, adhere to the codes inscribed in stone outside of the great temples of the journalistic art. In other words they were going to try to be very self-righteous. And incredibly dull.

Which is exactly what happened. They went on, not enough people watched, and soon they were running after our stories.

We did not abandon our old standards. There was a nice
Michigan story in which we really showed our stuff. A married
woman in Flint had been having an affair behind her husband's
back. Eventually, she broke it off and went back to her husband. Her lover, however, was unwilling to let it go at that.
He had made some rather explicit home videos of their torrid
sessions together, unbeknownst to her, and was not shy about
showing them around. He began hounding the poor woman
with copies of the videos, trying to force her to rekindle the
ashes of their affair. He sent copies to her home, to her husband, to her neighbors, to the local PTA.

Naturally, we heard about such goings-on, and David Lee
Miller was soon on a plane with strict orders from Brennan
not to come back without a story and the tapes. Miller made
it to Flint, got copies of the tapes in some devious manner, and
now had to mislead the crew from *Inside Edition*. Disguising
his voice, he called their hotel and told the reporter that he had
a copy of the tape and that he was willing to turn it over,
provided that it would be used in a fair and nonscandalous
manner.

The reporter agreed. It would be handled with taste and
discretion.

Miller had one more stipulation. Flint was a small town and
he could get in trouble if it came out that he was the source
of the woman's exposure. The reporter understood. Miller said
he wanted to meet on Saginaw Island. Miller had a map in
front of him. It showed the remote island in Lake Huron in
detail. Miller had taken the trouble to call the island beforehand, and so he knew a few facts about where the post office
was located, where the stop signs were, and where to find an
open hotel.

He told the *Inside Edition* reporter to get a pencil and a

pad, and he gave him very explicit instructions. You get off the ferry and drive to the second stop sign and make a left at the Texaco station. . . . It sounded very authentic. Only a native would know such details, thought the *Edition* reporter. Then Miller gave the reporter the most pertinent part of the instructions: "Wait there for my call."

The *Inside Edition* reporter followed the instructions to the letter. He checked into the hotel and waited for the call while we put the piece on the air. Every once in a while Miller would call the hotel and say that there'd be a hitch, and it was too late by the time they caught on.

Chapter
Fifteen

WE were prepared for 1989. The hungry challengers were coming at us, assuming that we were a flabby, out-of-shape champion, but they would find instead a lean street fighter. Gerald Stone had taken over from Ian Rae, and he had an inclination for hard news. He told us that he had liked the breaking stories we had done in the past, and that we should do a lot more of them. Only we would do it in our own peculiar style. We were not going to shrink from sentiment and emotion, our bread and butter—after all, we didn't want to lose our livelihood—but we would translate the cold recitation of bleak facts into human drama. It would be an amazing transformation.

Stone was just the man to do this, since he had the twin backgrounds—an American with long Australian experience. He appreciated the value of solid research as well as the tang of gut feelings. If Rupert wanted to invest the show with dignity and energy, he'd picked the right executive producer.

In late January a convention of television syndicators met in Houston, and one of their panels was devoted to reality programming. The producers from Geraldo Rivera, Sally Jessy Raphael, and Morton Downey Jr. were supposed to be there, and me, but because of the shooting war with *Inside Edition,* I couldn't leave town. They put me on a great Oz-like screen, and I rose to the occasion to defend tabloid television. I reminded everyone that the best tabloid was jolting and caught the attention of a slumbering public. Somehow the notion had come about that news was church business and had to be uttered with ponderous and humorless reverence; instead news was a circus delivered by clowns and dancing bears and should be taken with a lot of serious skepticism. I reminded them of what we had done with Mary Beth Whitehead and Robert Chambers and the Taylors and James Richardson, and said that we on tabloid television had been able to accomplish things that no one else in the entire medium had managed to do. And, besides, even old Joe Pulitzer, in whose name we conferred our highest honors, had run the biggest tabloid newspaper in New York City.

The virtue of the tabloid approach was proven again later that year in two stories that marked milestones for us. Gerald Stone wanted us to get out and become a kind of blue-collar version of *60 Minutes,* for which I was very grateful. The truth was that I was getting cabin fever from sitting behind a desk. The only time I got out was to hit the road for promotional tours to sell the show. But Stone expanded our writ. This was to be the year that we established a real claim on serious as well as playful journalism.

* * *

Stone made his first important move in the summer of 1989. On the afternoon of July 19, a little after three, Brennan called me on the set during a commercial break. "Come to my office when you're done," he said. I could sense the kinetic force in the office when I came off the set. Brennan's face was cold. "There's been a plane crash in Sioux City, Iowa," he said. "Go."

A United Airlines DC-10 en route from Denver to Chicago with 296 people aboard had plowed into a cornfield after losing an engine and suffering total hydraulic failure, leaving the aircraft with no steering ability. It was a terrible tragedy, but what made it an exceptional story was the news that 184 people had survived the cartwheeling crash that had left a three-quarters-of-a-mile gash in the earth. There were bound to be accounts of heroic rescues and miracles, as well as moments of profound sorrow: a microcosm of human behavior under tragic circumstances, which was always the best kind of story.

Our staff was scattered about the country, but this was the signal we'd been waiting for. Mike Watkiss was pulled off an assignment and chartered a Lear jet. Mike Squadron, a field producer with a lot of CNN background, went with him. Maureen O'Boyle dropped a story she'd been working on and threw some underwear in a bag. John Johnston was also on the rented plane.

David Lee Miller was in Starke, Florida, covering a story about the fight to execute a man who'd been accused of setting fire to his entire family. Miller had been driving in a rental car when he heard the news about the plane crash on the radio—he always kept tuned to an all-news station. He called Brennan from his cellular phone and Brennan said, "Go."

Miller drove to Gainesville, then flew to Atlanta and on to Chicago, where he rented another Lear jet and flew into Iowa. He met Watkiss and Squadron at the Sioux City airport later that day, and by the time he'd arrived, Watkiss had already done a story about some of the rescues and outlined others. Watkiss was new to the show, taken on after the bleeding to *Inside Edition* and *The Reporters,* but he proved himself in Iowa.

I landed in Omaha, drove one hundred miles north to Sioux City, opening up my rented Ford and speeding over one hundred miles an hour across the flat Midwest countryside. When I got there, I was bowled over by what Watkiss and Squadron had already accomplished—besides the first interviews, they had also rented two choppers and had Maureen O'Boyle up in the air, duplicating the flight path of the plane.

We were quick, but as usual we were late. The networks were swarming all over the field, and a media center had been set up for press conferences. Brennan had hired crews from Oklahoma City, and after driving all night, they were there, too, in a truck, which we parked near a fence at the airport. In the background were the smoking pieces of Flight 232. It was our first time out en masse, but we didn't miss a beat.

Watkiss found a man wandering around the field and started talking to him. The man turned out to be a retired DC-10 pilot who was searching for a friend in the muddy field. The retired pilot's name was John Shattuck and his friend—another pilot named Paul Burnham—had been hitching a ride to Chicago. Burnham lived in Denver, and Watkiss convinced Shattuck to call the missing man's family and agree to be interviewed. As soon as David Lee Miller landed, he went off to Denver.

Burnham's wife, Karlee, was stoical and bit back tears as she spoke of the lot of a pilot's wife. "It comes with the territory," she said, her eyes welling up. But the grown daughter, Stacy, made the segment. She told Miller that her father had always preached that planes were safer than cars. Then David asked her, "If there was something you could tell your father, what would that be?"

She was quiet for a moment, and then began to weep softly. "We were never a family that communicated a great deal," she said. "I never had a chance to tell him I loved him."

Watkiss also found a Norwegian exchange student who'd survived the crash. Gitten Skanes was celebrating her eighteenth birthday, and the bittersweet moment of her survival and the tragedy combined was visible on television. The celebration and sorrow wafted in the air like heat waves.

He found three children who had been riding the plane alone and had been plucked out of the burning fuselage, uninjured: the Roths: Travis, 9, Melissa, 12, and Jody, 14. Their mother, Leslie, had flown in frantically from Denver after hearing that only two children had survived the crash, but she found them all unhurt at the home of Luanne Gruber. Mrs. Gruber was one of those solid, no-nonsense, Midwest types. She'd taken the children into her home because they had just gone through an ordeal, and she didn't think that they should spend the night in some kind of institutional setting. "I walked by the rooms every once in a while to see if they were having nightmares," said this staunch woman, who, when asked why she had done such a thing, said simply, "I would want someone to help me."

Her husband, Roger, nodded.

She had also opened up her home to another couple who had been on the plane. A good woman.

I sat on the roof of the truck and interviewed Shattuck, who was also out of the Midwest soil, another deeply dependable soul who spoke about what had happened and speculated about how it had happened. As we were sitting up there, waiting for the satellite, I noticed the people. They kept coming in their pickups. Wearing their International Harvester caps, they came up to the fence and stood there and just watched. They were silent and respectful and even the babies didn't cry. It was eerie.

It must have been like that during the dust-bowl days, when silent, stoic farmers watched the land blow away helplessly. They came because tragedy was part of life and they were obliged to pay witness.

After it was all over, we went to a restaurant and were surprised when people began coming by the table, paying their respects. I hadn't realized until then how much our show was appreciated in the heartland. They understood something that many of our critics did not. We were Iowa's *60 Minutes*.

I drove back to Omaha and made the mistake of trying to catch a few hours' sleep at an airport hotel. At two in the morning they never close up, and the sounds of the engines kept me awake. I caught a six o'clock flight back to New York.

Gerald Stone had been right. We had reached a turning point. In spite of the technical glitches—and we would always be bedeviled by trying to hit the satellite—we could nail down a hard-news story in the style of *A Current Affair*.

Less than three months later we proved it again. Connie and I were at a dinner party being given by former Senator Abe Ribicoff and his wife, Casey. We had gotten to know the Ribicoffs in Washington when he'd been a senator from Connecticut, and they'd befriended Connie and me when we'd moved to New York—shown us around town, introduced us to good restaurants and their friends, and generally acted as hosts. It was sometime after eight at night, and I was wondering about what was happening in the World Series game, when a phone call came in. There had been an earthquake in San Francisco.

It was October 17.

We turned on the television set and saw that it was bad. I started hunting for Brennan. You don't just call Brennan's office. Tracking him down takes a hunter's skill. I started at The Racing Club, and yes, he had been there. I called Fortune Garden, and he had been there too, but, no, he was gone. Then on to Alexandra's, and Nichol's, and The Beach Cafe, heading north, as if he is making his way home, bar by bar. Brennan was always a moving target.

I caught up with him at some wet oasis and he got on the phone in that calm, controlled voice, and said he had heard about the quake. "Mate, we're already on this," he said. "You better get going."

He had a Lear waiting for me at Teterboro Airport in New Jersey.

David Lee Miller was in Wausau, Wisconsin, working on a story called "The Dairy Princess." A girl who worked at a Dairy Queen had murdered a Homecoming Queen because they had both been in love with the same guy. With that alert ear of his, he had heard about the quake and found Brennan, who'd told him to get out to San Francisco. Miller phoned his friends at Lear rent-a-jet and told them to have a plane fly from Chicago to Wisconsin. Miller already had his tape crew with him, Dick and Theresa Fisher of Berlin fame. Dick put the $12,000 fee on his American Express card. The Lear people asked if David had any catering demands, and Miller, knowing that Dick was a vegetarian, told them to have some cracked-wheat bread aboard the plane.

The plane was late. After an hour and a half, Miller called Lear and asked why the delay. The rental people said that the crew was all set, the plane was ready to go—but they were having a hard time finding cracked-wheat bread.

"Forget it!" howled Miller.

They flew into San Jose because the San Francisco airport was closed, rented two helicopters, and went to work.

As it turned out, my Lear jet had engine trouble and I had to abandon the trip. If I'd switched to a commercial flight, I would have missed the broadcast, and it was better to anchor it from New York than miss it entirely.

Brennan was already at work on the promos. We knew that we could not compete with the vast network coverage, so he decided to focus the show on a small stretch of highway in Oakland where the death toll was high and the rescue efforts were epic. It was a two-level highway, supposedly earthquake-proof, that had collapsed on itself: everybody's seen the pictures of it. The cars on the lower roadway had been crushed by the southbound lanes. Brennan had already dubbed it "The Last Mile."

David found a fireman, Lieutenant Bill Jarret, who had been crawling in and out of the small spaces between the two roads on Interstate Highway 880. He had seen people crushed in their cars, and a surviving child whose leg had had to be amputated so that he could be dragged out and saved. It had been too late for his parents, who were still in the car, dead.

The fireman, his face caked with soot, his hair plastered to his scalp, told how he had lain in gasoline and worked to free trapped motorists, and when the firemen had left the scene to get heavier equipment, they had been booed by the residents, who misunderstood and thought that they were quitting. It was a painful thing for him.

I sat in the studio in New York and wrote and rewrote the opening, choking back my own emotions at the terrible stories.

"The earth moved and time stood still," I began, as music in the background played "Welcome to the Hotel California."

There were always stories in contrast. Miller found a sculptor named Don Rich, who, even as he volunteered to go back again and again to the elevated highway, planned a monument to the victims. The sculptor told of seeing cars pulverized with gruesome bodies inside, then, a few feet away, a BMW empty and untouched. The owner had locked it and put on the alarm system and walked away.

Brennan was right to have taken a small strip of highway and focused our coverage. We knew that we could react to the bell. And we would prove it again in Berlin.

Meanwhile we continued to do our old brand of stories, too, especially those that punctured pomposity. Who could resist when the target was so big? When Donald Trump and his wife, Ivana, had their much-publicized marital tiff, it invigorated everyone, the sudden and jagged decline of the man everyone referred to as "The Donald." The Donald, you'll remember, was having a none-too-discreet affair with a model named Marla Maples, and at a ski resort in Aspen, Ivana told the other blonde in public to keep her mitts off her husband. This eventually led to a separation and a war of dueling press agents as to who was the more culpable, complete with hot stories about prenuptial and postnuptial agreements providing Ivana with $25 million, which she claimed was not enough to support her and her three children. (It took a while and a recession for us to catch on that Donald, like a lot of straying husbands, couldn't afford to play around.)

Through some devious means or another we obtained an exercise tape that Marla had made, which showed her jumping up and down in a clinging sweatsuit, bouncing and jiggling like mad. Every time we mentioned Trump, and we made certain to mention him a lot during that period, we showed the exercise tape. When the story moved on from a billionaire's love triangle to the crumbling of his financial empire, we showed the tape again, the bounce and jiggle now appearing emblematic of his downfall. It was like our version of a Passion Play.

We inferred early on that Trump might be having some financial problems, too. The next day I was getting a haircut and the phone rang at the barbershop. It was Trump. Calling me at the barbershop!

"Maury, you're way off-base. My businesses are in great shape. The casino revenues are up in all my places. I'm sending over my latest reports. You'll see. I'm in great shape."

And then he threw in the strangest farewell: "We'll get together soon. Oh, by the way, you know why your wife was so tough on me a few weeks ago when she interviewed me? It's because she did a lousy job with Marlon Brando, and she was trying to recoup her image."

And with that, he hung up.

Months later, while plugging his book on the *Joan Rivers Show,* he jumped on Connie again, criticizing her as an interviewer and bringing up the Brando story again.

Later that day Fox News in New York caught up with me on the street and asked me about what Trump had said. I replied, "Donald should worry about his bondholders, not my wife." By then we all knew what kind of "great shape" his business was in!

We had no end of the stories. There was the one about the Detroit man who was a district attorney by day and a priest by night. There was the Florida woman who had been the state's most prolific burglar until she'd been caught. Then there were the twin mayors—identical twins in Smyrna, Tennessee. Sam Ridley had been the mayor until he got caught selling police cars from his Chevrolet dealership. He then resigned and his brother, Knox, took over. In the town of 11,000, no one could tell the difference. They dressed alike, they talked alike, they acted alike. They both claimed to be mayor. And they were both right.

Such stories, which were plucked like folklore out of the police blotters all across the country, kept up our popularity. We were flying high, and no one higher than me—and then the earth came up to meet me with a resounding crash.

Chapter Sixteen

*I*F there is a bright and sunny side to this business, there is
also a dark and ugly undertone. It's not just the usual
ambitious toads who rise to management in every company.
It's not even the ordinary corporate atrocities committed
against the innocent, which one can expect. Television is a
high-stakes game, played by rough characters. And we do not
always know what we are up against. I was about to come
face to face with a nightmare. It would affect my whole view
of television news.

As I've mentioned, in my gypsy days, during my cup-of-
coffee in Chicago, the senior anchor was Ron Hunter, a man
who always reminded me of Ted Baxter. Journalists with ink
on their hands were all terrified of seeming like Baxter, that

archetype of the self-absorbed narcissist created on *The Mary Tyler Moore Show,* so they went out of their way not to act like him. Of course there was a little bit of Baxter in us all—had to be, just to be in the business—but when it went too far, the sensible ones were awakened by irreverent crews who knew the weak spot. Not Ron Hunter. He was a boyish man of roughly my age who bore a physical resemblance to Tom Brokaw, and had a policy, almost a pride, about never going out on stories. It left him with a reputation for being shallow.

Roger Ebert told a story about me and Hunter once in that period when I worked in Chicago. I chased the ambulances and would check in every night with the assignment editor, an old newspaper hound named John McHugh, who would find a good story for me to work. McHugh was none too fond of Hunter, as an anchor or a reporter. Seeing that my willingness to go out on stories gave me a reputation as enterprising and made me popular with the troops, Hunter decided to try it. He came into the office one evening and asked McHugh, "What have you got for me tonight, John?"

John looked over the rim of his glasses and replied, "Utter contempt."

Nevertheless, for reasons that are complicated and buried in my own insecurities, I liked Ron Hunter. He came to me when I was suffering under management oppression, and expressed solidarity. All anchors feel this sympathy for one another. Every one. We have all been screwed by management. We will all be screwed again by management. It's only a matter of time.

There is one other unutterable truth: In the end, all anchors suffer the same fate. Sooner or later you will be fired or turned away or let go, or whatever euphemism they wish to put on that cruel act. No one stays forever. So we know that in spite of the fame and glitz and big salary, all anchors have been dealt a bad hand.

Thus, when the Chicago management tried to make me do the noon news, and he came to me and whispered, "Don't let 'em get to you," maybe it didn't mean much—but it meant something.

Besides, I was no threat to Ron Hunter, which is a rare thing. You take two white male anchors and put them in the same newsroom and there is a great possibility of war. We were very different, however. I hung out with the reporters and he went home to his apartment, where he had a big-screen television set and watched his newscasts being replayed. I couldn't stand to watch myself.

During my ordeal he invited me up to his apartment, turned on his oversized set, and sat there drinking bourbon and branch water, watching himself. He was dating a nurse named Bunny, and she was a nice woman, blonde, robust, and completely submissive. Ron's career was the central feature of their lives. He worked for it, and she worked harder.

We lost track of each other for a while, but we kept in touch in the usual vague sort of way. I read about him or he read about me in one of the trade magazines, and word of mouth travels faster than the satellite pictures. I knew that he had left Chicago and was in some kind of professional downward spin. I assumed that it was nothing alarming, just one of the regular, built-in dips in the media roller coaster.

Three years later, when I had gone through Los Angeles and San Francisco and had come to Philadelphia, he came to the Westinghouse station where I was now his senior. He worked the noon news and his status was clearly reduced. Being senior is nothing that slams you in the eye—a larger office, an automatic deference for the best story—but it is very well defined by television means.

Ron didn't seem to mind. And he hadn't changed. He still spoke as if he were on the air. Ron was all television, scripted and pancaked and presentable. Bunny was always worshipful and handy. And that was when it first struck me that Ron had not changed. He was exactly the same as he had been in Chicago, only a little more weather-beaten, as if he had had no personal experiences along the way. It was a chilling but not unique story.

He and Bunny were married in Philadelphia and most days I would see them around the station together. She seemed uncommonly happy about finally settling him down, basking in his television fame.

He stayed in Philadelphia for a while, but he developed a bad reputation. They said that he was hard to get along with and that too often he anchored around the script, straying from the TelePrompTer. They said the same things about me, too, though, and so I didn't ascribe too much importance to the stories.

After a while Ron left Philadelphia and went to New Orleans, where I heard he had a big salary and a big job and lived in a big house. Bunny had two babies, and if I did not think about him much, it was because I was absorbed in my own fingernail climb.

I went to Washington and then to New York, and after *A Current Affair* clicked and went national, I started to get calls from Ron, who said his career was fine and that things were going great, he had great prospects ahead. And then he always asked if I knew of a job. I passed along his audition tapes and my recommendations to the management people, and the answers always came back the same: "We have nothing open at this time." That's always a lie, because if they wanted someone, they made room. The truth was that we didn't hire him because we were hiring kids and paying them peanuts.

He didn't sound desperate, but he didn't sound altogether happy, and I put the worry about him on the back burner. I was too busy with my own ride into space. He kept sending new tapes and I saw that he was trying to move into new areas, becoming a consumer advocate, an environmental advocate, a man with a mission. One tape showed him driving off a bridge to show how to get out of a car underwater. In another tape, he launched a campaign to get bulletproof vests for cops.

At the same time that I began succeeding, however, Ron began falling on hard times. In 1988, after yet another confrontation with management, he lost his news anchor job and wound up working for a radio station at night for five dollars an hour. This was a man who had been making a quarter of a million dollars in 1977.

I talked to my agent, who said he couldn't do anything for him, and I talked to Bunny, who always sounded a little strangled. Ron had not been a hit for a long time. He was difficult to get along with, everyone said. However, I knew that there were 200 markets and three stations in each market. All 600 stations ran three news shows, so there were 1,800 anchors in America. Somebody had to have a job for Ron Hunter.

At the 1990 National Association of Television Programming Executives (NATPE) convention in New Orleans, Ron called. He was the host and news director on an "all-information" radio show. He said things were going great, ratings were shooting sky-high, the station had just finished a huge promotion campaign and he was on his way back. He had had Jesse Jackson on the show and the Governor of Louisiana. Then he asked me to be a guest.

It was a Wednesday afternoon when I went to WSMB, a 5,000-watt station that sat in the shadow of the Superdome, and the studio was dark and very spooky. It had been built with bleachers for an audience, but there was no audience, and Ron and I sat in this massive, dark, empty studio and talked about old times in Chicago and Philadelphia. He laughed the way I remembered and looked the same, but we were in the dark and it was hard to tell how things really were with him. Then again, maybe he always kept us in the dark.

When I stepped outside, after the broadcast, it was six o'clock at night and dark, but compared to the darkness inside, it felt like the light of day. There was a mood not unlike the opaque menace of *Twin Peaks* inside the studio.

Bunny was waiting outside and we chatted in the parking lot, in the shadow of the Superdome. Things had been hard, she said. They had suffered and Ron had taken his fall badly. I tried to console her and said things would turn around—it was the nature of the business. She had one of her two children with her—I can't remember which—but I remember that the child's face was dirty. She said that she had left some things at my hotel—a pecan pie and a New Orleans witchcraft doll. I thought that she looked plain, like a mommy.

She asked me to come by the house, and I said that I couldn't because my schedule was too tight. I said that I would spend more time with her and Ron when I came back the next year.

"I won't be here when you come back," she said. "I can't take it anymore."

I dismissed it. I told her that something would break.

She shook her head.

Several months later I was reading the news wires when I sat bolt upright in my chair. There was a story about Ron Hunter. I read it twice, then again. It was the same Ron

Hunter. The story said that early that morning, Bunny Hunter, his wife, had committed suicide. She'd taken a .38 caliber pistol and shot herself in the chest while he'd lain asleep beside her in their bed.

When I got over the initial shock and the swarm of disbelief and denial, I remember sitting in that little station with the empty bleachers in the shadow of the Superdome, and then coming outside and talking to Bunny and her child with the dirty face. I thought about the hard thing that Bunny had said when I said I'd be back next year: "I won't be here."

I wondered if that was Bunny's suicide note.

The wire story said that the buildup to the suicide had taken place on the air. The day before, Ron had been interviewing Dr. Judith Kuriansky, a psychologist, about troubled relationships, and then started taking phone calls. One of the callers had complained about not being able to get close to her husband, who was distracted and disinterested. Dr. Kuriansky had advised the woman to do something to catch her husband's attention, to reach out and make some effort to arouse him and make him appreciate the size of the problem.

The caller then said, "Take your hand and push him off the chair: he's sitting two feet from you."

It had been Bunny. Her last cry for help.

Ron had laughed. I heard it on the tape of that last program. He'd tried to act as if it were a joke, or some light banter that was not serious. But it was serious. You could hear the nervous undertone in the laughter.

After reading all the wire service copy, I came out of the office blinking, as if I were walking into sunlight. People were going back and forth through the warren of desks and monitors, as they always did. There was the usual chatter and playfully insulting jokes. A normal workday at *A Current*

231

Affair. They didn't know Ron and they didn't know Bunny and didn't feel the awesome blow that I felt.

I yelled for Brennan, and asked if anyone was on the Ron Hunter story, and he said he had assigned reporters and field producers. I told him to back off. He didn't remember Hunter, but I told him that I knew the man and that I would call. He was a friend. No one should do this thing but me.

Not that I was even sure we should do a story. I did know that I should make some effort to reach him, as a friend.

The trouble was that I didn't have his phone number. Amy, my assistant, didn't have it either. He had always called me.

"Call the radio station," I told Amy.

Ron's substitute host came on the line and asked to talk to me. He wanted me to go on the air, as someone who had known Bunny and the family.

It was infuriating, and I felt the heat that all people in the public eye must feel when the press is breathing down their neck. But then I shook it off. Okay, I told the guy, I'll go on the air if you get Ron and ask him to call me. We made a sordid deal. I went on the show and talked about Ron and Bunny and what a tragedy it was. No one could have guessed that she would do away with herself in a fit of despair. She had been a sane, normal woman who'd had a grasp on reality.

Ron called me back within an hour. He was composed. I was a wreck, and kept saying that it was unbelievable, but he sounded as if he believed it. The memorial service had been held and she'd been cremated after the tissue and blood samples had been taken by the coroner.

"Why would the coroner take fluid samples?" I asked.

"They're sending them to the FBI for analysis," he replied. "There are routine toxicological tests in a suicide."

That sounded reasonable. And then he said something that I ascribed to shock: "My career is in big trouble."

I knew that this business was odd and did strange things to people. After all, I sat at a desk behind which was a larger-than-life picture of me used in promotional ads. We lead larger-than-life lives in this business. We are bewitched by our own fame and it should not have been so surprising that he was thinking of his career at that moment of surpassing crisis. We are conditioned and trained to be self-absorbed.

Almost as an afterthought he said that the police were giving him a hard time. They were not prepared to declare it a suicide. There had been some scandal there lately, with a cop who had shot himself and a screwup in the autopsy, so they were conducting investigations on all sudden deaths.

"What?"

He said there was still some doubt about her death. The circumstances were unclear to the authorities.

That set off bells in my head.

"You have to get a lawyer," I said.

"I've got to deal with this," he said. "I'm on leave from the station."

"You've got to get a lawyer," I repeated.

"No." He sounded stubborn. "I'm not hiring an attorney. I did nothing wrong."

"That's not the point. The point is, when you get into legal trouble you get legal advice."

"I'm not getting a lawyer; that's all there is to it. I answered all the police questions. This is a classic case of suicide. That's what they told me. The night she killed herself, the cops said it was a classic case."

In the next two or three days we talked often. He called me at home and I called him, and we even spoke about the possibility of his coming on *A Current Affair* to tell his story, but the timing seemed wrong and I felt ghoulish pushing the issue.

Finally, at the end of the week, I was on the road when I

got an urgent summons. It was Ron. When I called him back, his voice was completely drained of emotion. He said that he had been fired by the station. The manager had taken him to the cafe in New Orleans' Pontchartrain Hotel and told him that he was off the air. He was gone. His seven-year-old daughter, Alison, was sitting at the table at the time.

"Not only does she lose her mother, but she has to watch her father being fired," he said.

It sounded strange, but I wrote it off to the pressures of his plight.

"Would you call the owner of the station?" he asked.

"Of course," I replied.

I was truly outraged. No matter what he thought, the owner had some human obligation to stand behind his employee. Even if Ron was guilty of something—and I was certain that he was not—he should be given the benefit of the doubt.

I called the owner and I could tell in the first ten seconds that I had come up against a wall. I pleaded, saying that the man had just lost his wife and had two kids to support, and that it was not fair. Ron was supposed to be presumed innocent and was entitled to the backing of the station. I was highly indignant and let it show.

The man said, in a hard, immovable voice, that the matter was settled.

"Look," I said, "just as a matter of public relations, don't you realize how this makes you look? How unfeeling? How unfair?"

He said that he knew.

"It's a lose/lose situation," he said.

The man had made his calculations and was prepared for the bad publicity. After all, he said, the station had lousy ratings anyway, and Ron was too controversial, the show didn't work, and there was resistance from the advertisers.

Ron had always said that the ratings had been good and the feedback great, but he had that upbeat salesman quality and it was hard to tell when he was whistling in the dark or telling the truth.

The station owner spoke in a hard monotone. His mind was made up.

In all the years I have been broadcasting, I remember only one time that someone was rehired after being fired. It was at the CBS station in Chicago. They'd let a weatherman go and there was a big outcry from the public. The station hired him back and took out full-page ads in the newspapers saying, HE BEAT THE BOSSES!

But this was a done deal.

I called Ron and said I'd tried, but that the owner would not budge. Ron was fired and that was that.

Ron said he wanted to go public with this outrage and that he trusted me. He would do it on *A Current Affair*. I went down to New Orleans to do the piece myself. Field producer Teri Whitcraft met me in New Orleans, and by the time we had hooked up, she had made contact with the district attorney and the cops. Teri was a young woman who shone like a star behind the cameras. She was dogged and smart and knew her way around everything.

That first night before we went to Ron's house, she said to me that the story was not as clear-cut as it seemed. There was a bad history to the marriage. Ron Hunter had been accused of beating Bunny. Teri had found witnesses. They had been separated twice and had had many screaming matches. This had not been the first time that Bunny had used the station air to try to reach Ron. After the last call the station manager had warned Ron not to be abusive to Bunny, and calls had been made to the house to check on her condition.

"Maury, it's *Chinatown*," said Teri. Jack Nicholson's

movie passed through my mind, too. What was the truth? What was fiction?

When we went to Ron's house the next day, I was shocked. The Jaguar was gone and so was the splendid lawn and the expensive home. He lived in an apartment near the projects on a street called Felicity. He seemed . . . preoccupied. He sent the children to the next room and Teri went to play with them. We talked in the bedroom where their mother killed herself. The place looked like the aftermath of a college party, with Coke bottles and empty packages of cake.

I had already done the opening: "New Orleans is one of my favorite towns, but I don't want to be here. Not for this story. For this is about two friends of mine."

We had already gotten some tape of the studio whitewashing the billboard with Ron Hunter's name on it. Teri had done an interview with his replacement host, Michael Creasy, who had said the station heads thought that Ron should have cut Bunny off the air when he recognized her voice—that had been his real sin: bad judgment.

Then Ron and I got ready for the interview. He went into another room and changed and put on some makeup. I didn't have any makeup.

When he sat down for the interview, he struck the angle, the one I remembered from our anchor days in Chicago and Philadelphia. He moved his head so that the camera caught the good side. During the interview I asked tough questions about what had happened, and he said that he and Bunny had not argued that night, as some had said, and that he had simply gone to sleep, with the help of a sleeping pill. He had been awakened by a bang. Not a very loud bang. He described it as the sound you might hear when someone

236

mashed a paper cup, and he slammed his hand on the table. I know that I flinched. Then he had looked over and seen the blood on Bunny's chest.

Teri spoke to Ron during the break. She said that he seemed to be in a state of shock, that he sounded unemotional, numb, detached, that his true feelings were not coming out. During the next segment, he wept.

After the interview was over, I asked for videotapes and pictures of Bunny, and I took them when he gave them to me. We hugged and I wept myself. Later, when Ron was vindicated by the coroner, when all the verdicts were delivered and marked "suicide," it did nothing to help Ron Hunter. He was still out in the cold.

The show suffered from balance, so we showed the other side—the woman who had taken pictures of Bunny's injuries, the replacement host who had said that everyone had worried about Bunny's welfare after she'd called the show. We showed the tapes of Bunny playing with the children, and the wedding pictures. We showed Ron in his younger and unmarked days. And we slipped in disclaimers, as if lawyers were running the show.

I just couldn't be the friend with unqualified help.

Later a lawyer representing Ron called and said Ron was dead broke and could he be paid for his *Current Affair* segment? When management turned him down, the lawyer called me back and said that they were setting up a fund for the kids, and I sent a check.

I passed around his tapes and made a few calls, but I was never completely certain where the friend left off and the professional seeker began. The replacement host put me on the air for Ron's phone number. Ron gave me a story for a job recommendation.

Was it any wonder that Bunny could not take this business for one more second?

It had become too surreal for me.

On the plane home, I had a drink and then another, and I thought of that large studio and the empty bleachers and the quick slips in our business that come like air pockets when you don't expect it. I felt exhausted—with myself, with *A Current Affair*, with broadcast news. It was time to move on.

Chapter
Seventeen

IT had actually been coming on for some time now. It was in the middle of 1989 that I believe Rupert lost interest in *A Current Affair*. We all had the feeling that he was no longer watching. He had done what he wanted to do—beaten Roger King. *Inside Edition*'s ratings were nowhere near ours, and David Frost had long since left as the host. Rupert had just bought *TV Guide*, launched a huge satellite television operation in England, and had other fish to fry. He was more interested in the Fox Television Network than one syndicated show.

This made possible something that would change my life. Rupert and Fox had said again and again that our show was "story-driven," that the host was unimportant. I didn't agree, but I had always been wary of forcing the issue. It was Connie who told me that now was the time.

It was ironic in a way, and related back to the unnatural demands of the medium and the fact that ours had been an unconventional courtship. Connie and I had been a television couple, hopping from city to city the way you cross a stream, from rock to rock. We had been absorbed and obsessed with ratings and business gossip and the cruel battle with one management after another. We hadn't had time for weighing emotional priorities. We were jet pilots on red alert. We had a bag packed and an up-to-date passport and a beeper connected to the office. We had been wed to our careers and we could not be encumbered with other obligations, lengthy explanations, and a balance sheet of regrets. That's what had killed my first marriage.

After she had left the Washington station, our paths hadn't crossed again until I'd gone to work in Los Angeles and my life was coming apart. Connie would bolster me, give me faith in myself, because we were friends long before we were lovers. She told me that I had talent, and when she told me, I believed her. It was, I suppose, the same quality that made her so endearing and accepted on television. You looked at that smile on that unique, gorgeous face, out of which came a rich and confident voice, which sounded, if you listened closely, like it was holding in some clever joke. America not only believed her, they fell in love with her. I would have been un-American if I hadn't as well.

When I was fired by rough managements, she told me that they were idiots; when I had doubts, she made me laugh at myself. And when I bounced around the country, she loved me. We had long, cross-country talks all through the nights, and we broke up and came back together, then swore that we would not speak again. We would slam down the phones, crying on both ends of the continent, unable to figure out how it could possibly get any worse, vowing never to try again, never to speak to each other.

We fell in and out of love and kept going through circular fights about the nature and direction of our relationship. And then I would turn on my set and see her and I would have had to be made out of stone not to call.

We were television people, a media couple, and all the ordinary rules of engagement were twisted to fit the electronic evolution. The freedom had to be there to pick up and go when the story called. The long hours were factored in, because television is not an eight-hour day, and you cannot hold a television running back accountable for broken dinner dates and canceled vacations. And that fragile thing, ego, had to go. She was always my fan, however, and I was always her fan, and giving up an ego was a small price to pay for getting a personal goodnight from a woman who bid goodnight to America.

I understood the determination it had taken for her to succeed in this business. She had put her head down and charged ahead, and that required a single-minded, fierce attitude. Giving up that headlong plunge would be hard, and maybe even displayed some deeper love than I could fully appreciate. It was so hard and complicated that I knew she loved me.

We could not live together without being married. We both knew that. It was not the fear of scandal, but the deed of commitment that made it imperative.

And so we found ways. She finally called me on that day and told me that she had found the dress, and then called the next day and said that she had found a ring. She told her parents, who were relieved that their youngest daughter was finally doing something traditional, and I had to tell mine. I was a bit worried because, after all, Connie wasn't Jewish, but after I sat them down and said, "Listen, I love you both, but this thing is going to happen, with or without you," I realized that I should never have been concerned. They blessed us and the wedding was on.

We were married in New York City on December 2, 1984. There were only forty people there, and we stood in a bay window of our West Side apartment under a *chupa*—the traditional Jewish canopy—and took vows from Rabbi Balfour Brickner, who had married my brother and my sister. Connie had gone to see him to take preliminary instructions on becoming a Jew. Her family was Moslem, which was unusual in China, and she was accustomed to the unexpected. If there were children, they would be Jewish, and whatever was left of the family doubts vanished.

The marriage with Connie changed everything. I was certified as someone worthy. She had blessed me with her own indisputable seal of approval. And we became that sweetheart couple who didn't fool around or come out of the Betty Ford Clinic or come burdened with the usual backpack of failings with which celebrities regularly exhaust the public.

It also gave me bargaining power with Fox I had not counted on. I was no longer alone and reckless. I had Connie behind me, whispering, in her discreet fashion, that this was my moment. And it was. I was no longer reckless—I was dangerous.

After *A Current Affair* had beaten *Inside Edition,* I had gone back to Gerald Stone and renegotiated my contact, as he had said I could. He had given me everything I could have asked for—except for one thing. As proud as I was of what we had achieved on *A Current Affair,* there was something else I was itching to do.

I knew from my years on *Panorama* and points west that I could do a national talk show. I could elicit feelings and beliefs from reluctant guests. I could open up subjects that were considered too delicate. By now I had earned that craggy acceptability given to wicked uncles who tease forbidden subjects. Because of *A Current Affair,* and because I had mellowed and ripened and been through the corporate Cuisinart, I was certain that I could pull it off again.

My new contract with Fox gave me permission to talk with anyone I wanted about such a show, but of course it was at Fox that I wanted to do it. Hadn't they kick-started my career again? I owed them a lot, no matter how much they grumbled and continued to growl about story-driven shows and salaries.

I went to the Fox offices in California and pitched my idea. I wanted the show on during the day—night talk shows were a graveyard for hosts. I wanted an audience, because by now I recognized that audiences gave some atmospheric feedback that could not be duplicated in empty studios. In a pinch, a host could turn to the audience, like an ally, and call upon them for support.

They listened and nodded and patted me on the back, and I thought: This is terrific. We have an understanding here, the Fox partnership has been cemented once again. I was flying. And then something started to feel sour. They said that they would give me a talk show, and let me produce it so that I would have ownership, but it was difficult and we got stuck on small points. I did not want to negotiate *A Current Affair* with Ian Rae again, and so I wanted a clause in the contract saying that I would renegotiate future contracts in California. They came back and said that they would agree in the form of a letter of understanding, but that they would not put it into the language of the contract. And yet the letter never came.

I knew the party was over when I met with Barry Diller at

his Fox office and he congratulated me on the new talk show and wished for many years of *A Current Affair*. He gave me some good advice about the talk show: "Don't let the salesmen run the thing." Then he said, "There's a friend of yours here." In walked Rupert, who was charming and smiling and congratulated me, as well. Rupert and Diller started talking about the show—what time it would run, how it would play.

"Not nighttime," I said.

"Well, you should consider nighttime," said Rupert as if the whole thing had not been settled.

I was deflated and returned to New York in a state of growing anger and confusion. I thought these things had been settled and now we were back to square one. They had been debating time periods and technique and approach as if I had not even been in the room. They had been so smug and convinced. I came out of the session shaking my head.

That was it. In the emotion of the moment, it all coalesced for me—the years of running around, the vagaries of the broadcasting business, the increasingly cold attitude of the Fox brass, the feeling that no matter what I did there I would always be treated as just an employee—and I knew I couldn't do it anymore. I had to move on. Connie said: "Go for it."

I knew a woman at Paramount named Lucie Salhany, an attractive, dark-haired, TV-smart woman who had approached me to do a talk show. Lucie had great confidence in me and I knew Paramount was a big, focused organization with a terrific professional reputation, and I figured I might as well see what they had to say. I called Lucie and told her to come to New York and we would work out a contract. In two days we hammered out a deal that had lingered for months at Fox.

It was a bad week for Barry Diller. He had lost Jim Brooks, who had been under contract to him as well. Brooks had directed *Broadcast News* and *Terms of Endearment,* and had brought television respectability to Fox with a little cartoon character named Bart Simpson. I was a mosquito, but still, in Diller's eyes, it was another betrayal. He called me from Europe and gave me a blistering tongue-lashing, telling me that I was ungrateful. In spite of all the good and solid reasons I'd had for signing with Paramount, I was shaking when I went into Brennan's office and told him what had happened.

"This should be the happiest day of my professional life, and I'm drained and depressed," I said.

He waved it away and told me to forget it.

"It's business, mate. That's all."

I gave notice to *A Current Affair,* assuring them that I would live out the terms of my contract and work through May of 1991—and a sheet of ice came down on me from Ian Rae and his minions. Ian and Diller wanted to cut me off the air immediately, keep me unemployed and twisting in the wind.

Brennan, however, thought that we could use my exit to the advantage of the show. He suggested that we hold a year-long nationwide talent search for my replacement. Naturally, I would be the one to go out and conduct the search. One more upside-down gag to confront the critics.

I thought it was a brilliant idea and would take the sting out of the departure: A clear display of no-hard-feelings, mate. I would also get a lot of media play and make the show look good, as well as make the corporate side of Fox look human and endowed with something that so few corporate systems had: a sense of humor.

But the word from Rupert was a cold rejection. He did not want to call attention to my departure—he didn't even want to call attention to my presence—and he certainly did not want to create another media star out of my replacement. The man still wanted to maintain his idea of proper employee/master relations. And so I would leave with the usual public relations statement of insincere regret. It would be handled as just another formal expression of corporate babble: bad-news-disguised-as-good-news.

The anger was like smoke. They began bringing in replacement hosts, one by one, who were lively or indignant but did not sit quite right with Diller and his advisers. And then they brought in the undertakers. They closed the West Coast office and dropped members of the staff, and the handwriting was on the wall.

"It's time," Brennan said, and I called Lucie Salhany and she made him executive producer of *Hard Copy* with the stipulation that he would be available for consultation on my talk show.

When Brennan quit, Ian Rae acted like a deceived lover. "How could you do this?" he asked Brennan, and Peter replied with a look of such scorn that Ian could have turned to ashes.

A magazine editor was brought in to take Brennan's place, and she left a trail of strict rules and annoying instructions that smothered the ambition and spunk of those young, unbroken child producers and interns who provided the energy for the show. She held meetings and was crisp—a sharp and painful contrast to the lazy style of Peter Brennan, who would lean back in his chair and listen and listen and finally ask, in that heart-of-the-matter calm voice: "Who's the person we're rooting for in this story, mate?" To Brennan there always had to be a central character, a hero. There always had to be someone the public wanted to win.

The new managing editor remained locked behind her door and sent out harsh orders and, inevitably, the closed door and distant look suggested a style. Her office came to be called "the bunker."

There came a day when Raf himself let it be known that he was available for other work and Lucie grabbed him, too. Burt Kearns, the Berlin banana boy, was next, and then Gordon Elliott. After a mind-boggling diet regimen, he went off to become a game-show host as well as a guerrilla reporter for *Hard Copy*.

The kids came by my office, as they always did, and my office door was open with the odor of news, wild tales, and campfire stories clacking over the wire machine. But it wasn't the same. They'd broken up the team that had made *A Current Affair* soar and pop, and the life had gone out of the place.

About then the Ron Hunter story happened to me, and it only confirmed what I already knew: I had made the right decision.

It had been an exhilarating, wild time, a roller coaster ride through dark corners and gaudy spectacles, sideshows, and dramas, an adventure in making television history. And who knew? Maybe I was about to do it again. If *A Current Affair* had taught me anything, it was that nothing was impossible— and that nothing was impossible for me. I had Connie and my family rooting for me, and even more, I had myself. The wilderness would never claim me again.

It was time to go. I packed my bags.

They were lighter than air.

Chapter Eighteen

THERE were changes that last season with the show which I did not want or even notice. We became celebrities—something I found infinitely amusing. Connie and I were invited to important dinners and exclusive parties and rare outings. In spite of the fact that we are both natural recluses, we did attend one party at which Prince Philip was the guest of honor.

My mother, in her left-handed fashion, always said, "Is he not the most handsome man?" whenever she saw a picture of Queen Elizabeth's husband.

The last time I had met royalty was in 1978 when they were having a special piggyback Shuttle test landing at Edwards Air Force Base in California. I was roped off on the tarmac while this giant 747 came down. And far ahead of the press was Prince Charles, who was standing in the middle of the desert, where they had set up a glittering silver tea service. Inclement locales would not interfere with the afternoon tea of a royal guest.

Our host for the party in the spring of 1990 was Howard Stringer, who had risen high in the CBS network hierarchy. The affair was to celebrate the opening of Andrew Lloyd Webber's play *Aspects of Love*. There was a receiving line and we practiced respectful bows and hints of a curtsy and how, exactly, to address Philip—"Your Highness."

"I want you to meet the Prince," said Stringer, grabbing us under the arms and pushing us toward Philip.

As I got close, I whispered to Connie, "You know, he is good-looking. My mother was right."

Stringer pushed us in front of the Prince's handsome face.

"Your Highness, this is Connie Chung and Maury Povich," began Stringer, bending. The Prince smiled charmingly. "They are very big in American television."

The Prince's smile bobbed but didn't change. There was a moment of silence. Trained by television to move into dead air, I said: "You know, your Highness, I work for someone you may know. Rupert Murdoch."

The expression on his face went from complete charm to utter scorn. And then he said, "I guess some mug's gotta do it," and turned on his heels and walked away.

Connie and I looked at each other and burst out laughing. We had forgotten how rough Rupert's tabloids were with royalty.

On Thursday, August 23, I went out to California to pitch the new Paramount talk show to the Los Angeles stations. I had been going around the country with the chief Paramount salesman, Greg Meidel, and he would praise me to the skies, sometimes in a roomful of people who worked for stations that had, not very far in the past, fired me.

But now I was the golden child and the host of the "talk show of the nineties," according to Paramount, and the station managers listened respectfully because I had been given the credit for taking this little show, *A Current Affair,* and turning it into an industry. I was the glue that had held the show together.

When the managers and owners asked me how I would be different, I shrugged. Meidel would jump in and say that I spoke for the viewer, I got to the essence of the story. When the managers and owners asked me why I would be the logical host for the talk show of the nineties, I said, "Because this is the nineties."

Connie was with me in California. There was some anxiety at the time because of our decision to have a child. She had just told CBS that she had to lighten her work schedule, and cut back on her weekly show, *Face to Face With Connie Chung.* The network executives had been unbelievably supportive in allowing her the time off.

But how to make the announcement? Would the press understand? Connie and I talked about it for days. At first we thought, "Just tell them you're cutting back for personal reasons." Knowing the tabloids as well as we did, however, that would only invite more speculation—that there were cracks in the marriage, for instance. If she said it was for medical reasons, they'd have her at the Betty Ford Center.

We decided: why not tell the truth? We wanted to have a baby, and after seeing the doctors they had recommended an "aggressive approach," which meant cutting back on her field-reporting.

At the age of forty-four, time was precious. Connie was close to the wall for childbearing. I admired so much how she gathered her courage and set aside one of the most successful careers in television news to try to have our child. We had mused about it during the first five years of marriage, regretting, I guess, that we hadn't tried it sooner. No reason to look back now.

The story of her trying to have a child hit every newspaper and television set in the country.

We were stunned. We figured the industry publications might play it up, but from the *New York Times* to the *National Enquirer,* it was big stuff. The *Enquirer* even printed a story that said Connie was trying Chinese folk remedies, like hanging pictures of children all over the house and drinking a special kind of tea. Johnny Carson quipped during his monologue on his prime-time anniversary special, "Connie Chung was supposed to be on the show, but she had to cancel. Maury Povich has the night off." *People* magazine rushed out a cover story about Connie's decision, even though she declined to cooperate. It was a bit much. But Connie's decision didn't surprise me. When she went after something, particularly something this personal, she went after it heart and soul. Meanwhile, we were on the West Coast seeing medical specialists, and I took time out to see some station managers.

It was a glorious day, the temperature in the 70s, the sky clear, a miracle absence of smog, and I drove a rented car through the high metal Paramount fence on Melrose Avenue. I was struck by the blue skyscape, the size of a football field, a backdrop for an outdoor movie, that I came across when I passed through a gate. I knew that I had entered a fairyland.

I drove through the old lots where the bungalows of the forties were crowded with the ghosts of Steinbeck and Fitzgerald. I passed the sets of *Cheers* and the *Arsenio Hall* show.

We pitched the show and it went well and I felt a stretch of something. I walked around with my hands in my pockets, smiling like a tourist at the Art Deco style and the fake sky and the real sky and the bungalows where the writers worked on computers now. I found a long building, one of those prefabricated jobs, and it said HARD COPY above the door. I went in and asked the receptionist if Peter Brennan was in.

"Yes, Maury," she said.

"You expecting me?" I asked, surprised.

"I've been warned," she said, smiling. "Upstairs."

I walked upstairs, and there was a long corridor, and for a moment I couldn't move. I heard voices coming at me from the other end. I strained and listened. There was the rasp of Rafael Abramovitz, working his arguments like sandpaper. There was the reasoned hammer of Burt Kearns. And there was the lilting purr of Peter Brennan.

They were talking about a story. Penny Smart. A teacher in Massachusetts who had hired two students to kill her husband. It was our story! That is, it was *A Current Affair*'s story. We had reporters there. They had the tapes from local stations. It was locked up.

I stood outside and marveled. Here they were, in summer reruns, not even in competition with *A Current Affair,* and they were already biting and snapping and trying to beat us. I stepped into the doorway, where only Brennan could see me. Raf and Kearns had their backs to me.

"Why don't we ask Maury?" said Brennan, smiling.

Raf bristled. "Maury? What the hell are you talking about? He's in New York. He's loyal to that show. Maury? Are you crazy?"

"No, he's not crazy," I said. "You are."

They turned and jumped up and grabbed me. Then we all sat down, Raf in his cowboy hat, Brennan in his jeans, Kearns in an open shirt: Easterners, all-out, killer journalists of the nineties.

Now the question on their table was what to do about *A Current Affair*.

"We can keep them from using the tape," said Abramovitz. "We just tell the station that they can't give it to *A Current Affair* because they didn't sign releases and it belongs to us."

"That won't stop 'em, mate," said Brennan. "If it's news, we use."

I had heard that same argument a thousand times in New York when we had been blocked from using someone else's tape. Nothing stopped Brennan. "Maybe it's not ethical, mate, but it's legal."

"We tell the stations to lose the tape," suggested Raf.

Then Brennan said that he was going to open the show with an ambush interview. Gordon Elliott was going to grab this guy in the street and nail him with an interview on the run.

"Who?" I asked.

"You," replied Brennan.

"Oh, God," I thought, looking around at these transplanted media commandos. "Here we go again."

CELEBRITIES YOU WANT TO READ ABOUT

___THE DUCHESS OF WINDSOR: THE SECRET LIFE 1-55773-227-2/$5.50
Charles Higham
___LIFE WISH Jill Ireland 0-515-09609-1/$4.95
___ELVIS AND ME Priscilla Beaulieu Presley with 0-425-09103-1/$5.99
Sandra Harmon
___SUSAN HAYWARD: PORTRAIT OF A SURVIVOR 0-425-10383-8/$4.95
Beverly Linet
___PAST IMPERFECT Joan Collins 0-425-07786-1/$3.95
___LIVING WITH THE KENNEDYS: THE JOAN 0-515-08699-1-/$4.99
KENNEDY STORY Marcia Chellis
___MOMMIE DEAREST Christina Crawford 0-425-09844-3/$4.95
___MCQUEEN: THE UNTOLD STORY OF A BAD BOY IN 0-425-10486-9/$4.95
HOLLYWOOD Penina Spiegel
___ELIZABETH TAKES OFF Elizabeth Taylor 0-425-11267-5/$7.95
(Trade Size)
___LANA: THE INCOMPARABLE MISS LANA TURNER 0-425-11322-1/$3.95
Joe Morella and Edward Z. Epstein
___FATHERHOOD Bill Cosby (Trade Size) 0-425-09772-2/$6.95
___DANCING ON MY GRAVE Gelsey Kirkland 0-515-09465-X/$4.95
with Greg Lawrence
___MY MOTHER'S KEEPER B.D. Hyman 0-425-08777-8/$4.95
(Bette Davis's daughter)
___MOTHER GODDAM Whitney Stine with Bette Davis 0-425-10138-X/$4.95
___PIN-UP: THE TRAGEDY OF BETTY GRABLE 0-425-10422-2/$3.95
Spero Pastos
___I'M WITH THE BAND: CONFESSIONS OF A ROCK 0-515-09712-8/$4.99
GROUPIE Pamela Des Barres

The intimate, funny, and <u>true</u> story of a
Hollywood legend coming face-to-face
with her most ardent fan.

ME AND JEZEBEL

When Bette Davis Came for
Dinner—and Stayed...

by
Elizabeth Fuller

On May 28, 1985, star-struck Elizabeth Fuller's dream came
true when the legendary Bette Davis came to dinner at her
Connecticut home. Four weeks later, as the hotel strike in
New York dragged on, she was still there.

It's a Bette Davis no fan would expect: attending a neighborhood seance, river rafting, signing autographs at
McDonald's, and remaining every inch the superstar while
riding shotgun in a Toyota.

In one short month she conquered suburbia, took over the
Fuller's home and changed their life forever. For Bette Davis,
playing herself was a breeze. For Elizabeth, it was a perform-
ance of a lifetime.

_0-425-13264-1/$4.99